Greek
Mythology
Coloring Book

Adult Colouring Books

Aryla Publishing 2020

978-1-912675-78-4

www.arylapublishing.com

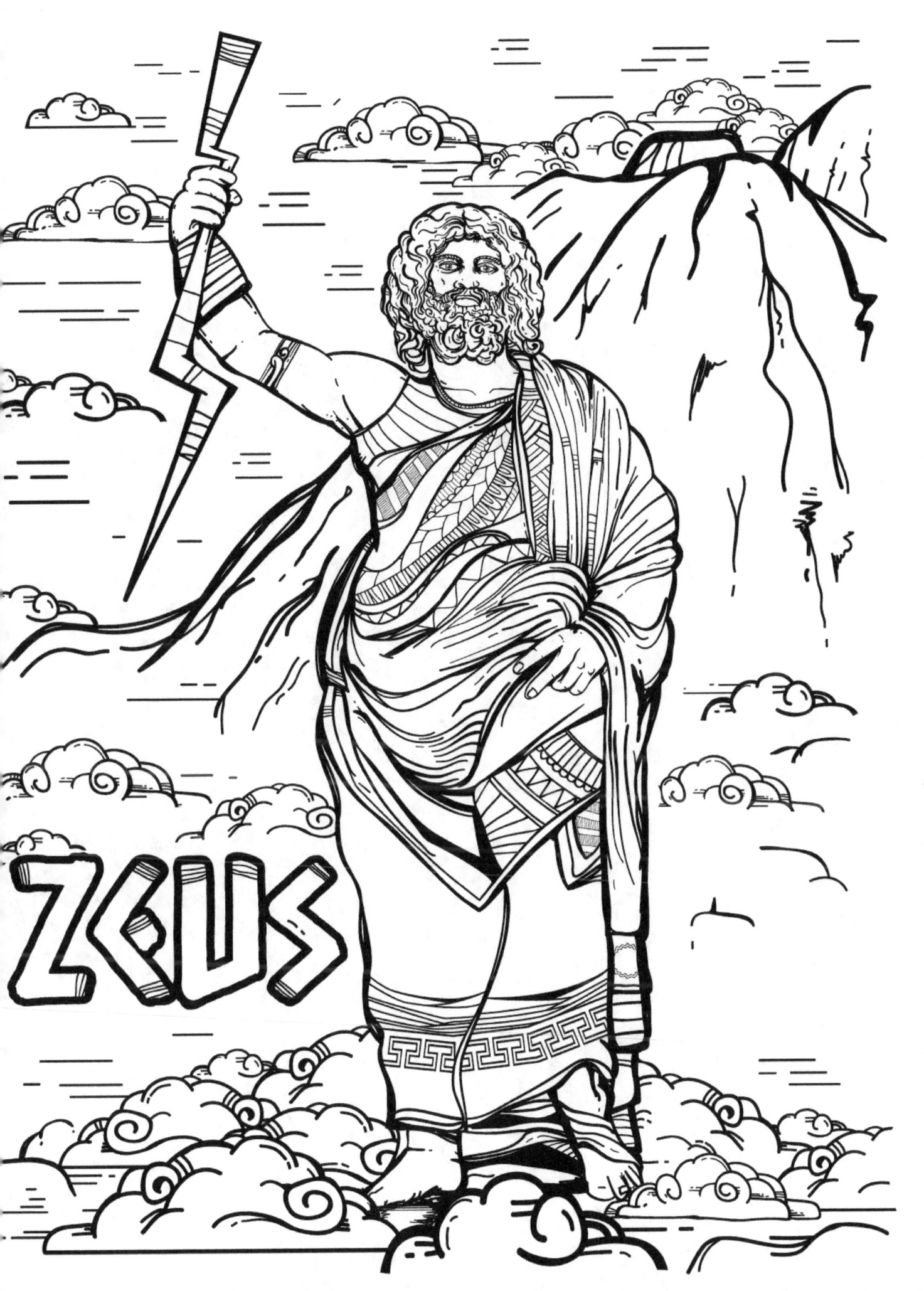

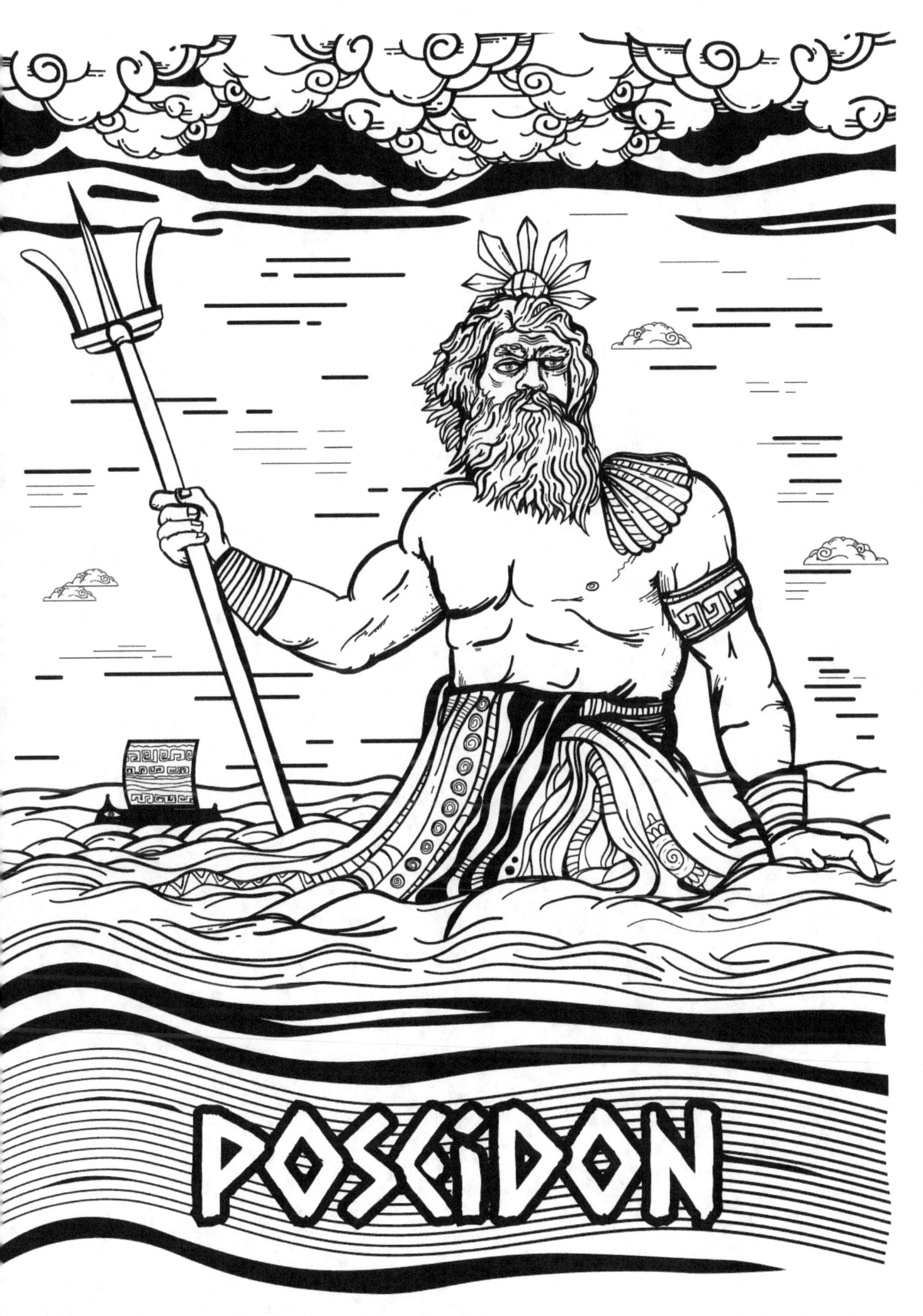

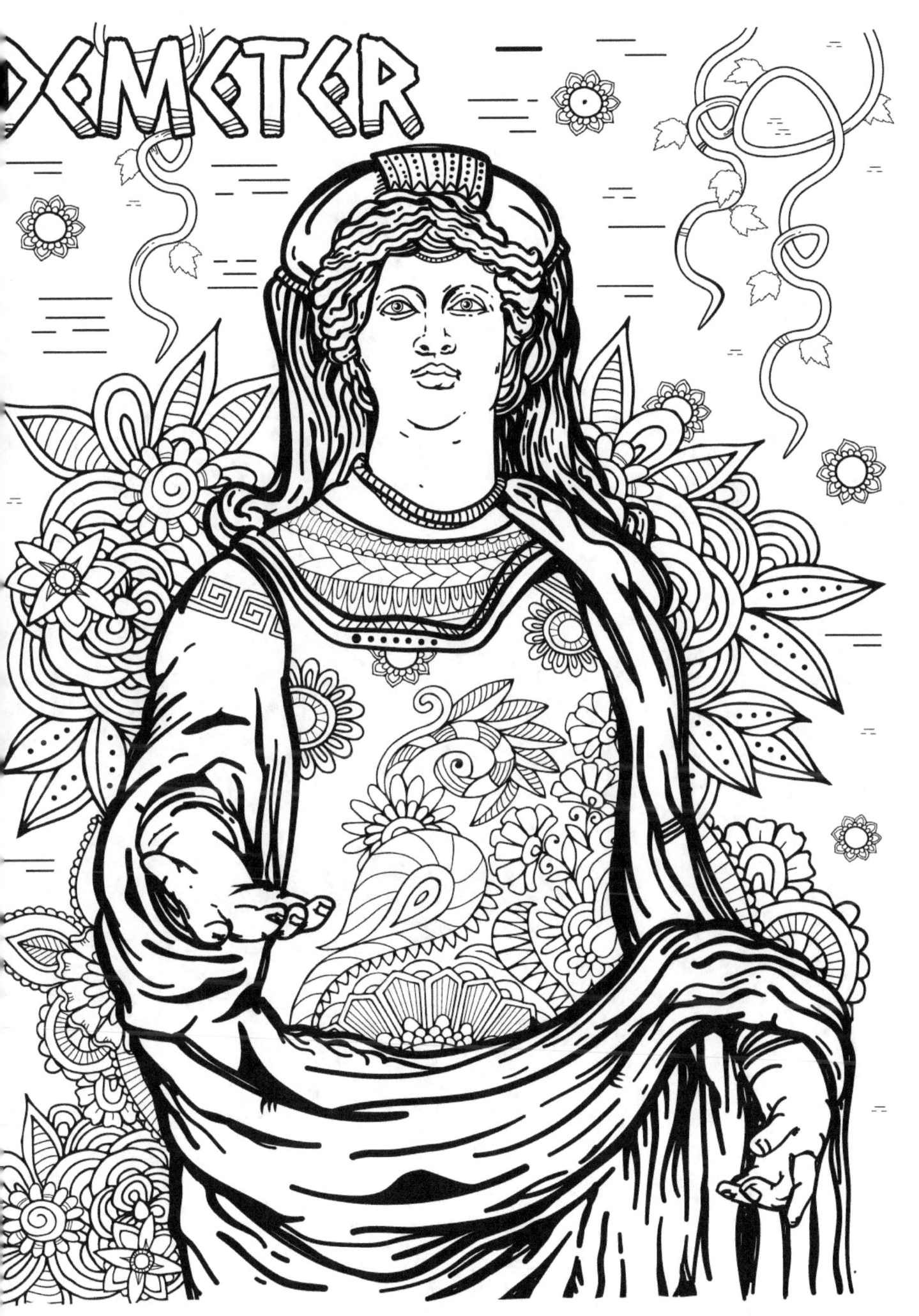

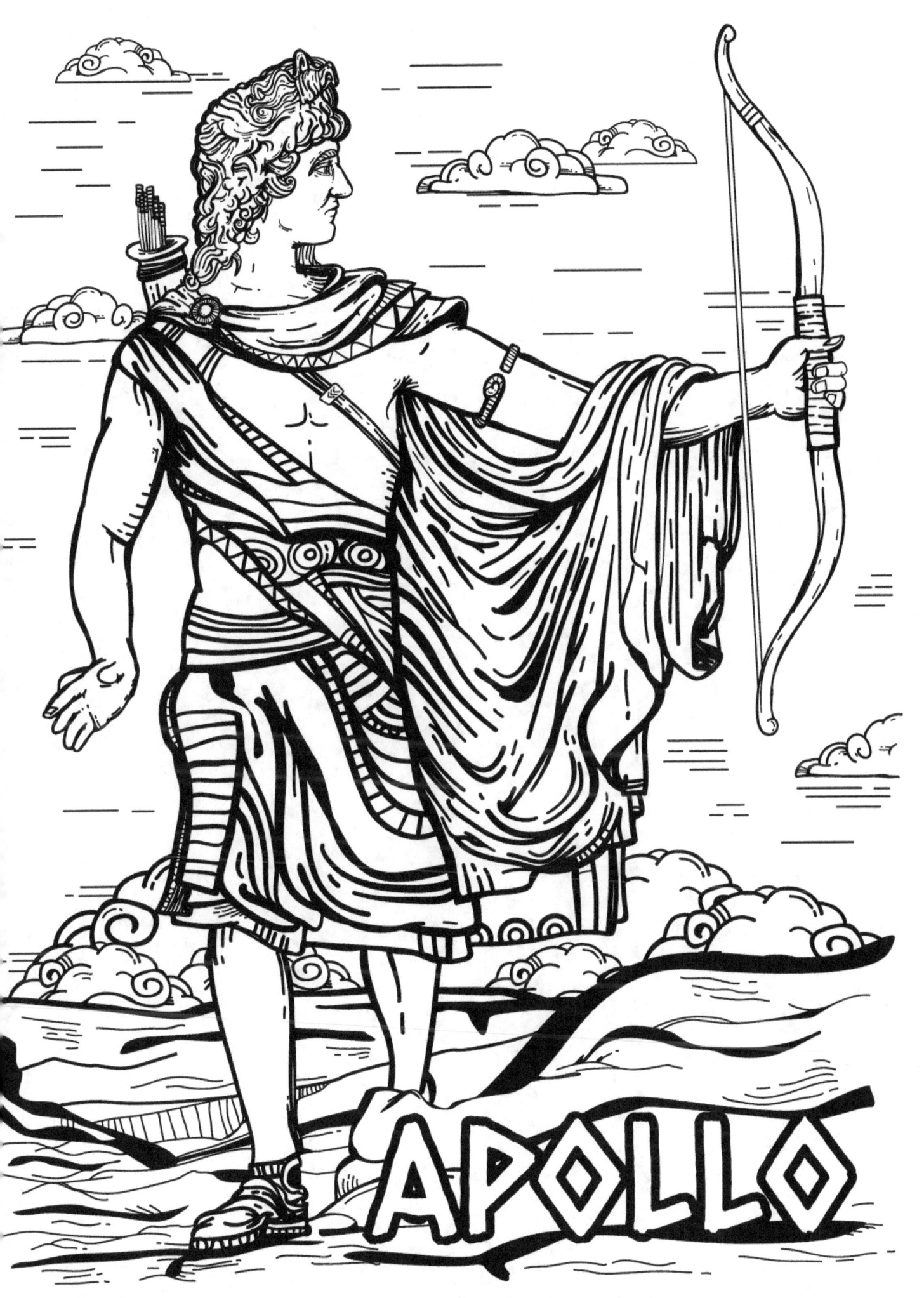

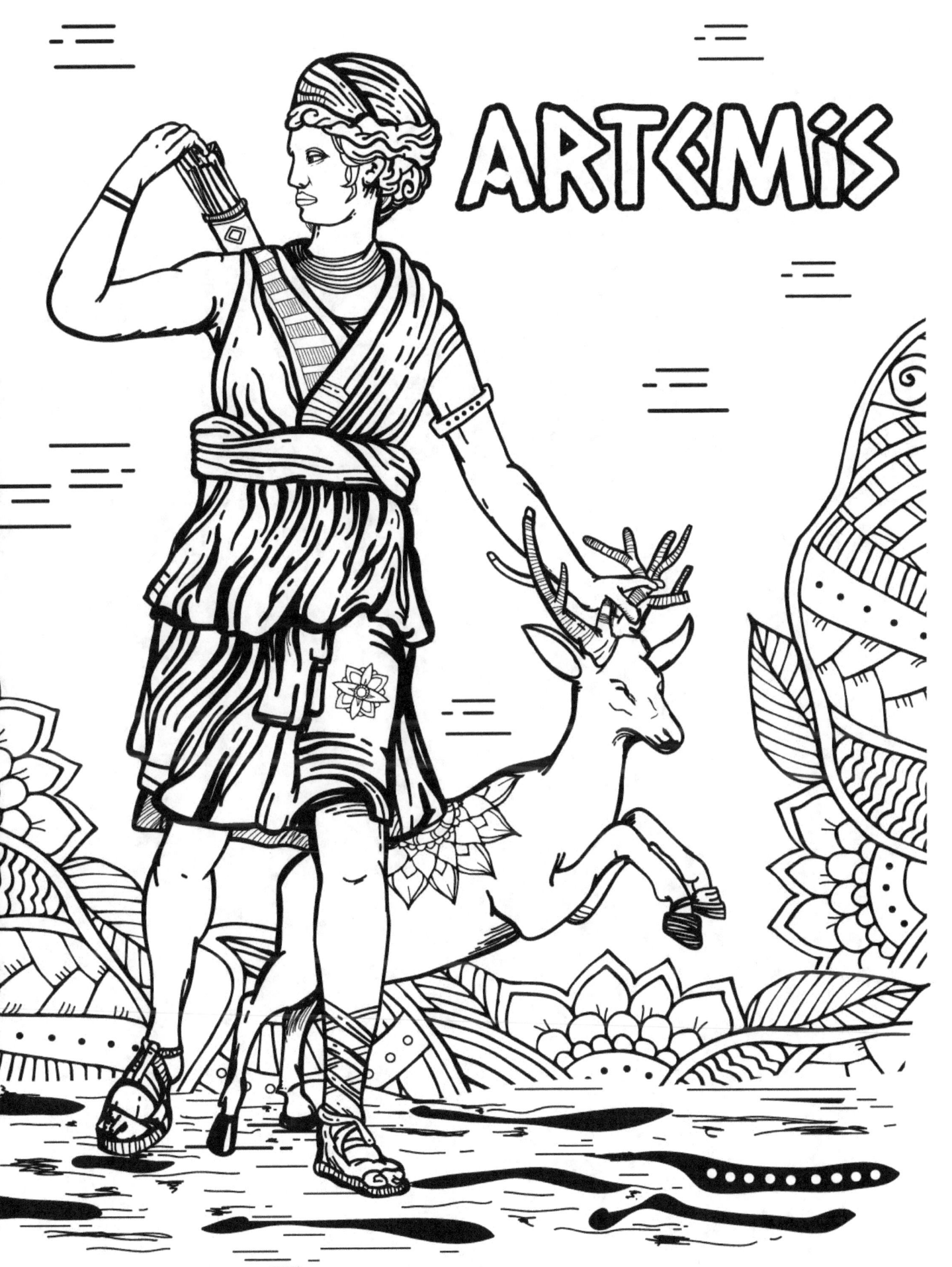

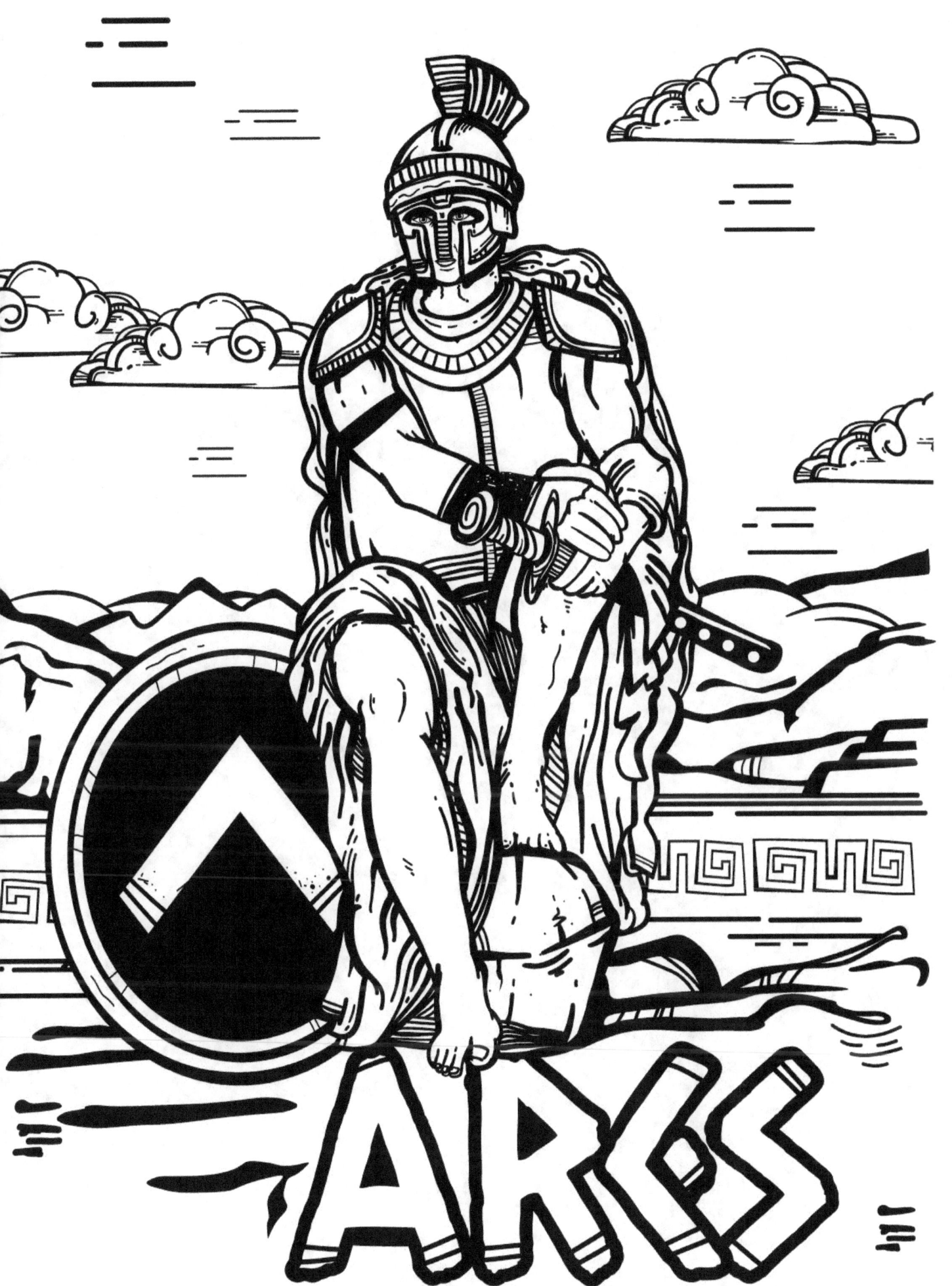

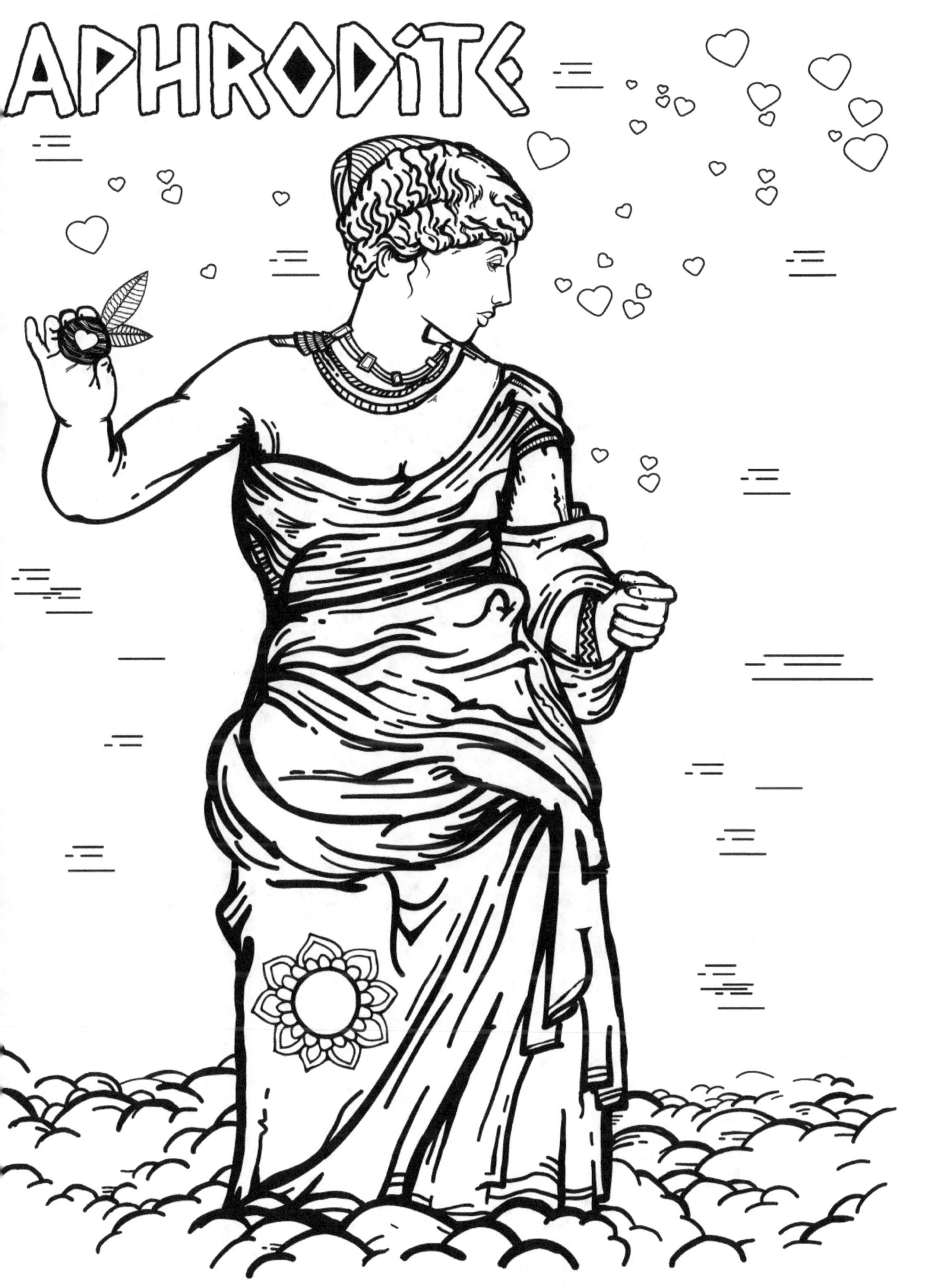

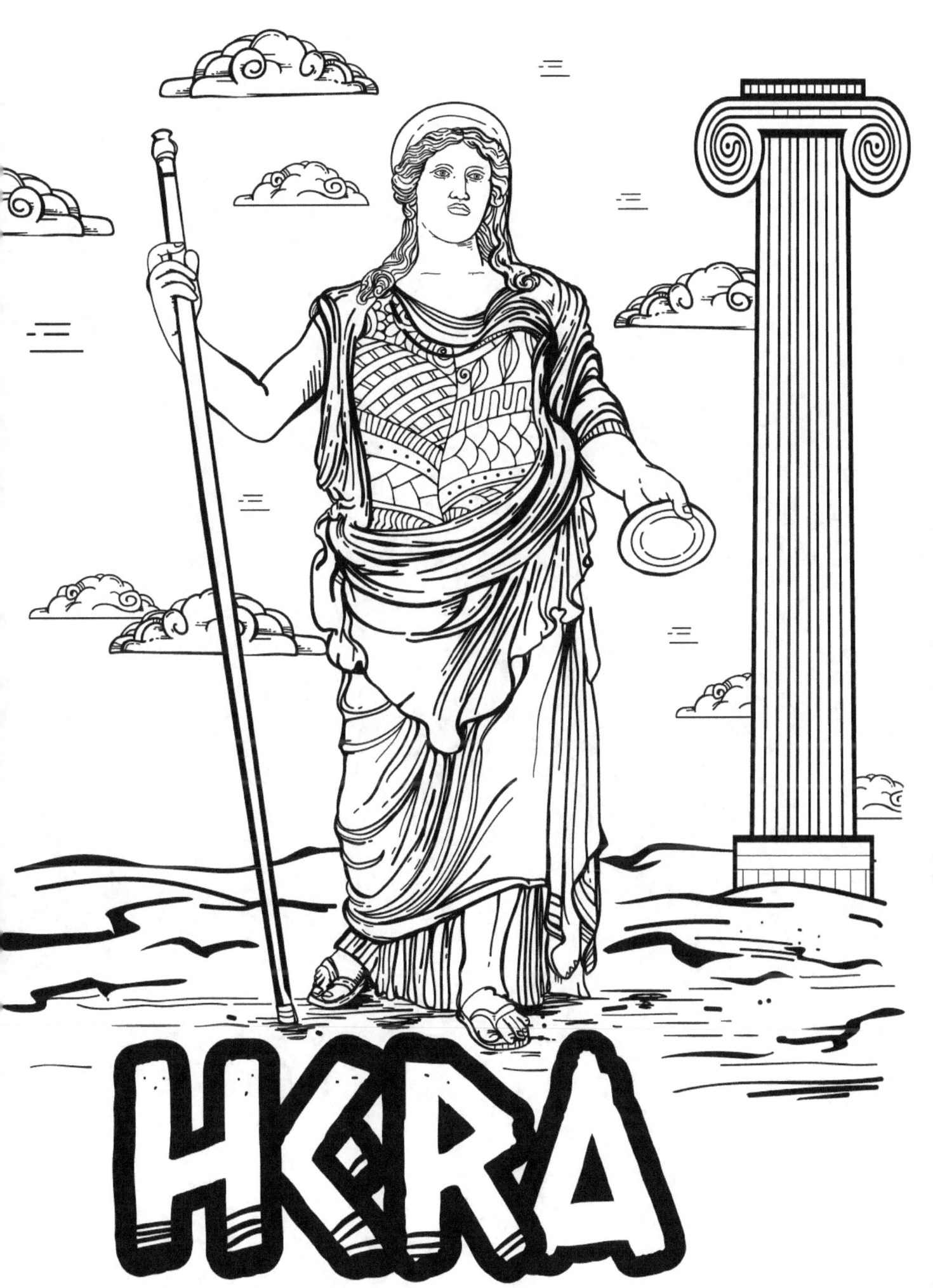

HERA

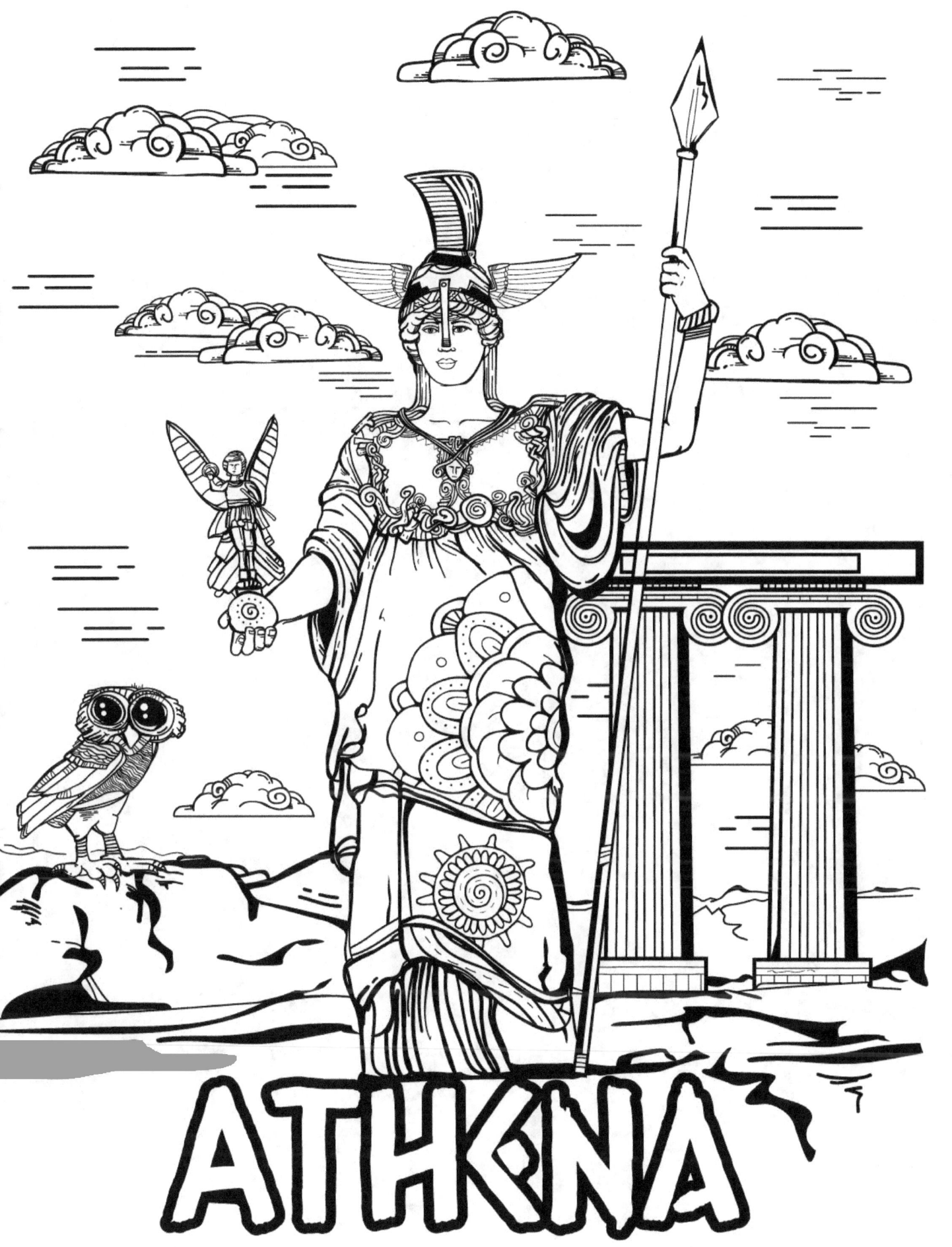

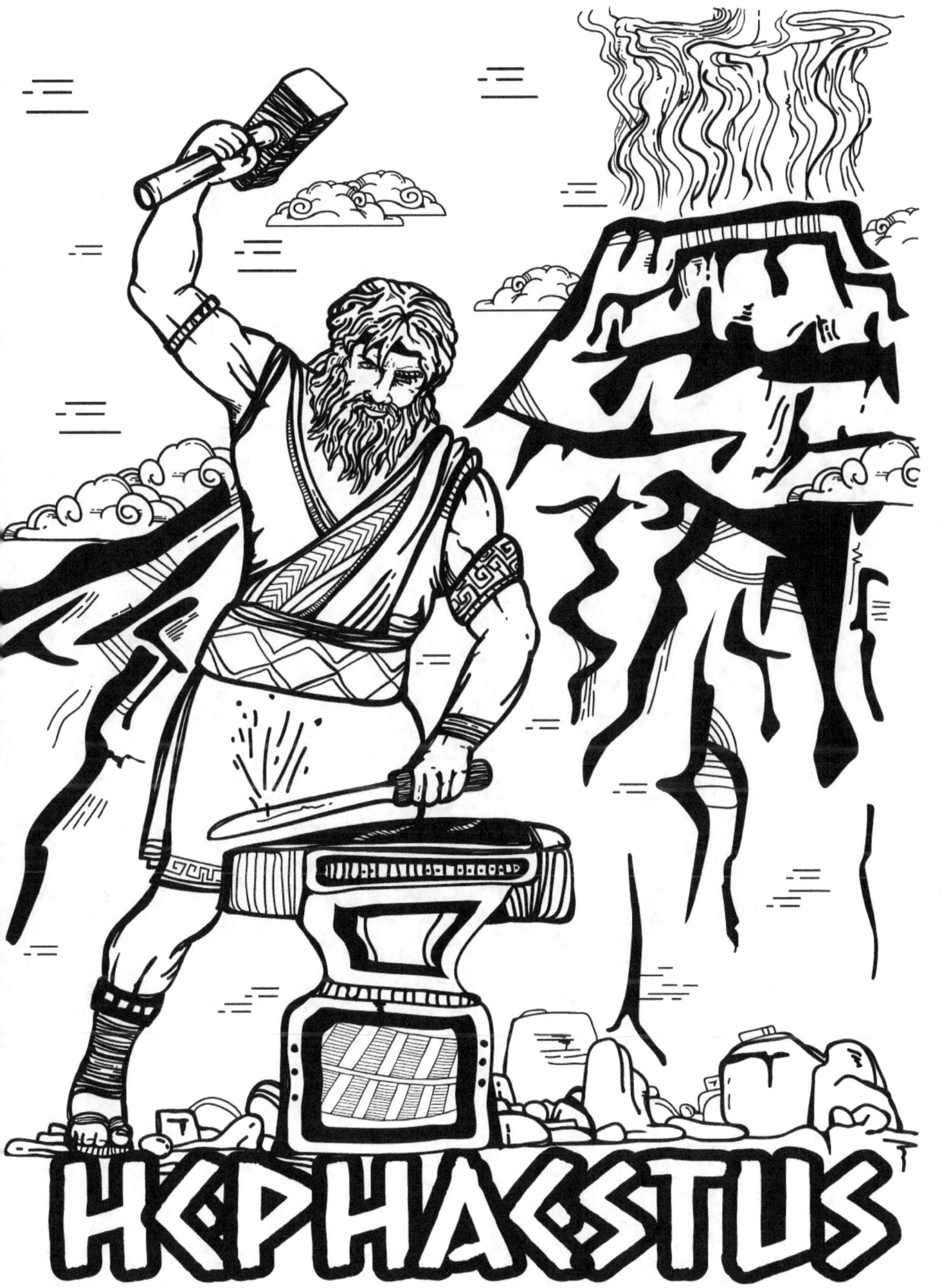

HEPHAESTUS

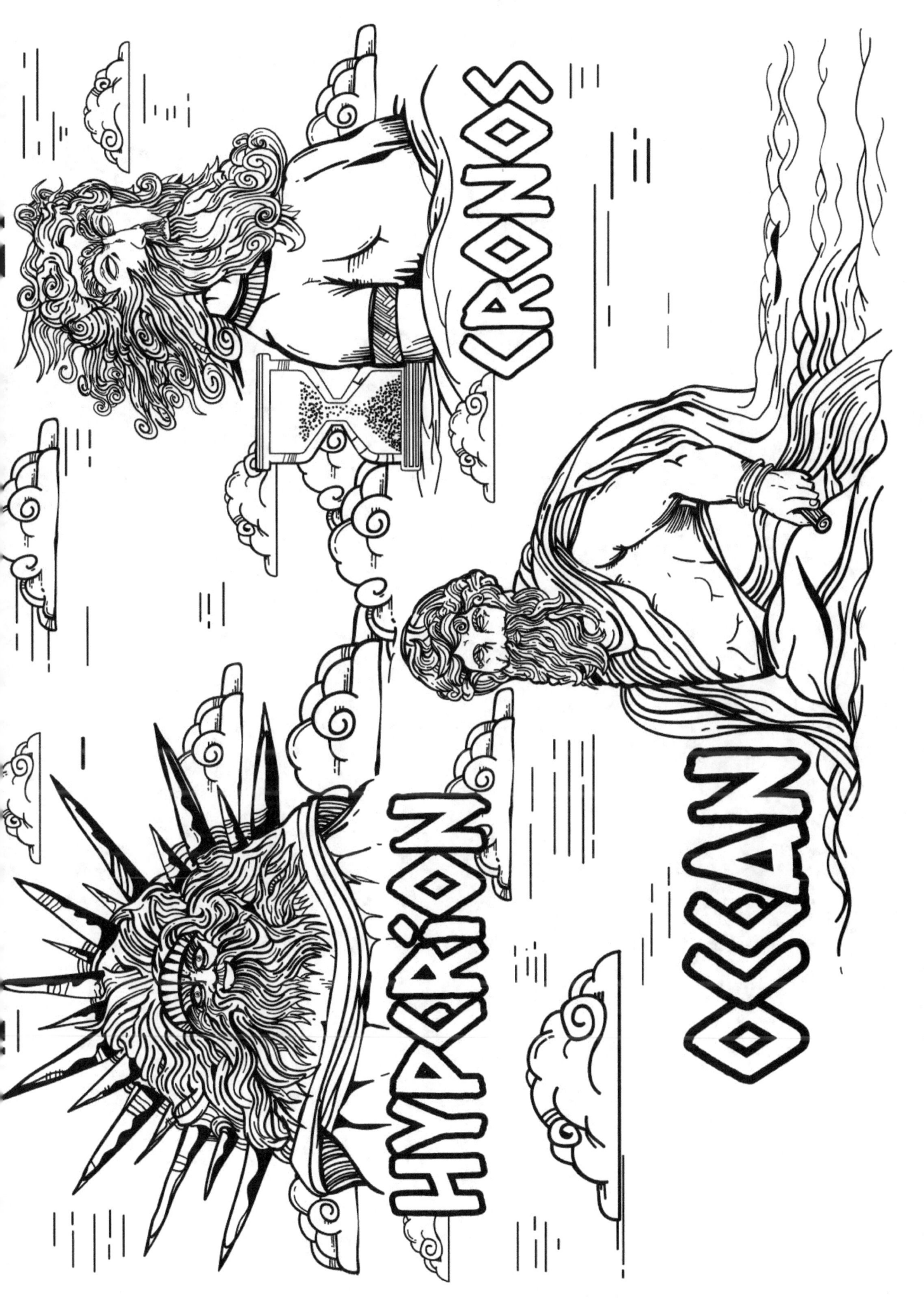

CRONOS

HYPERION

OCEAN

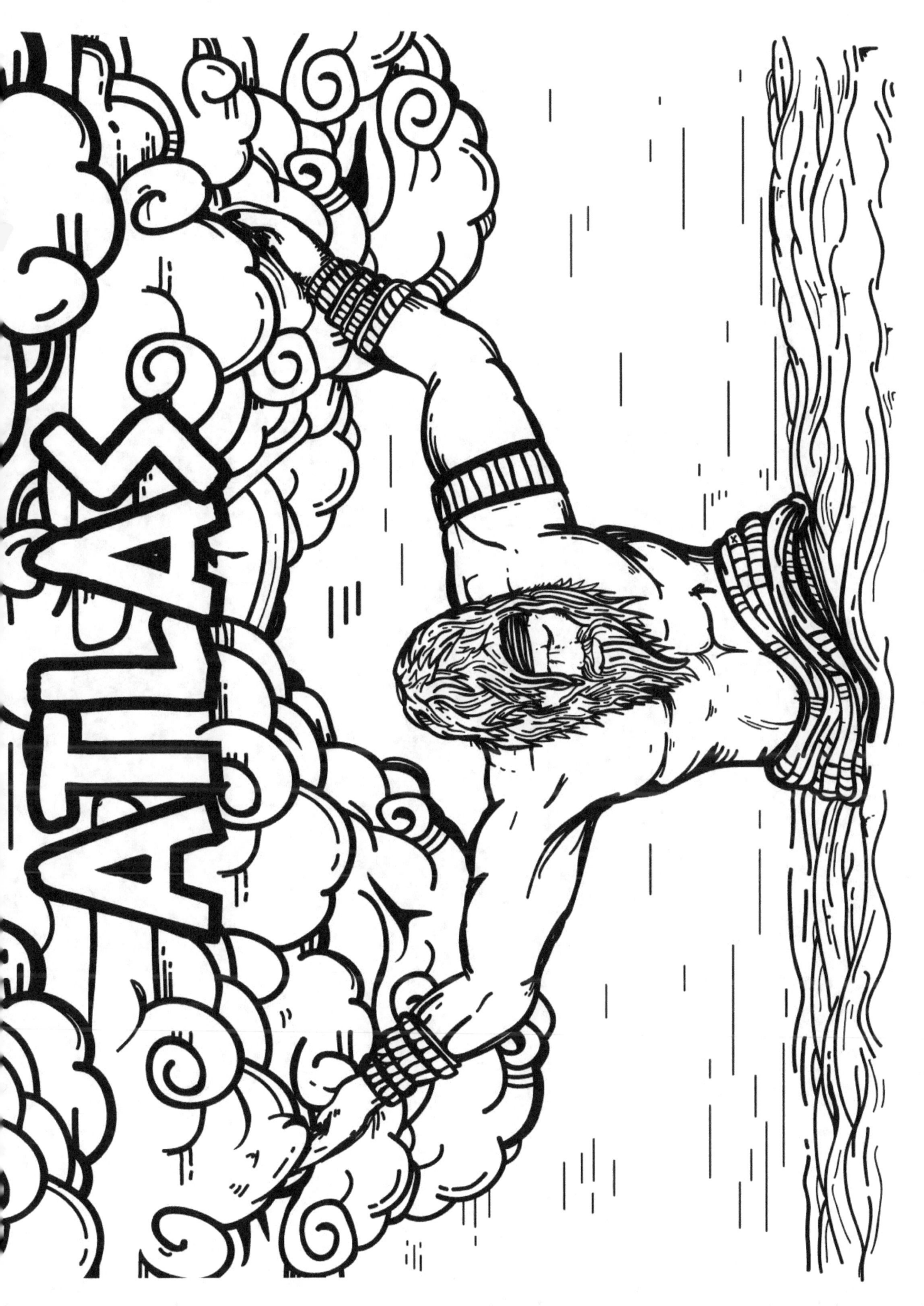

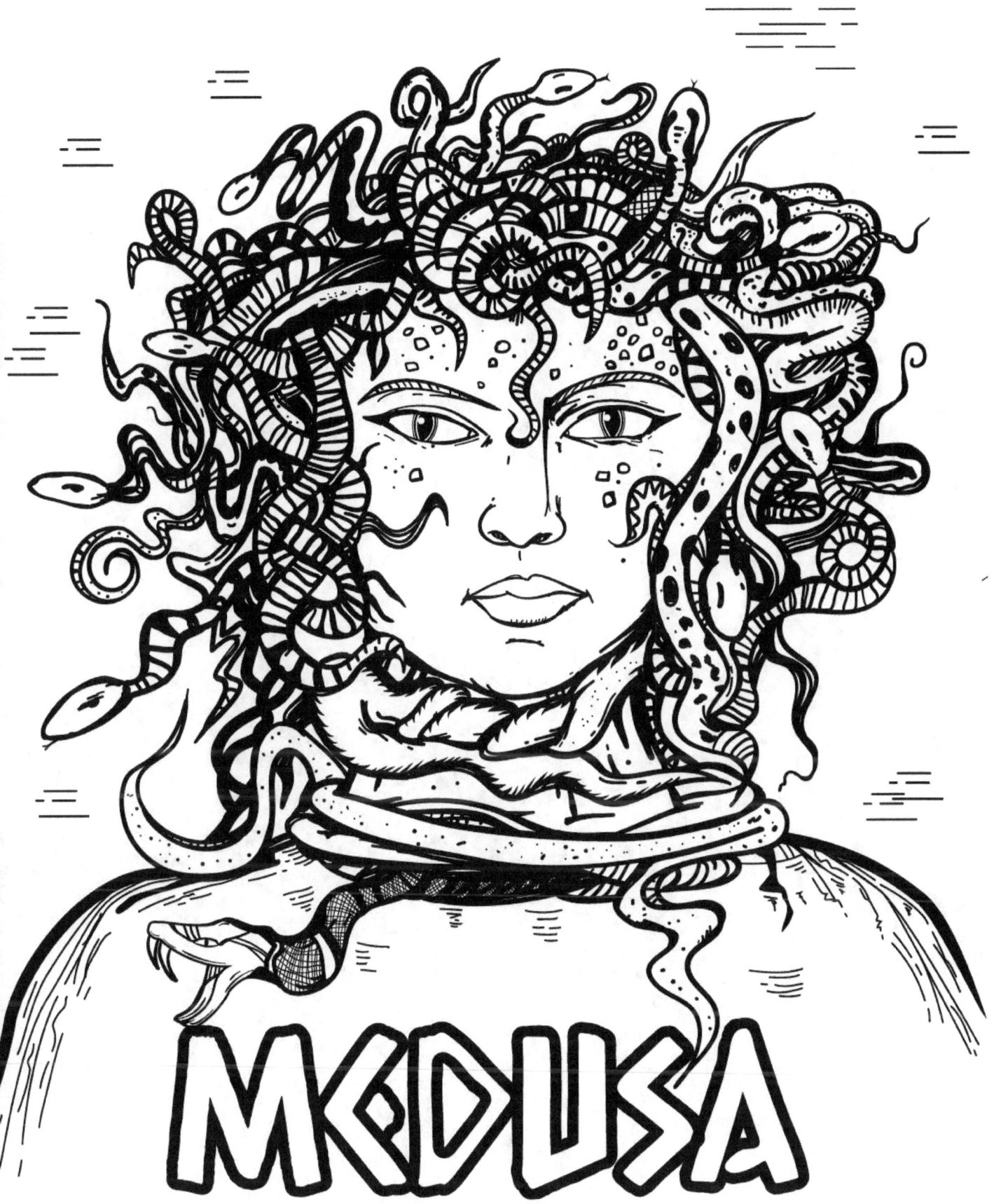

MEDUSA

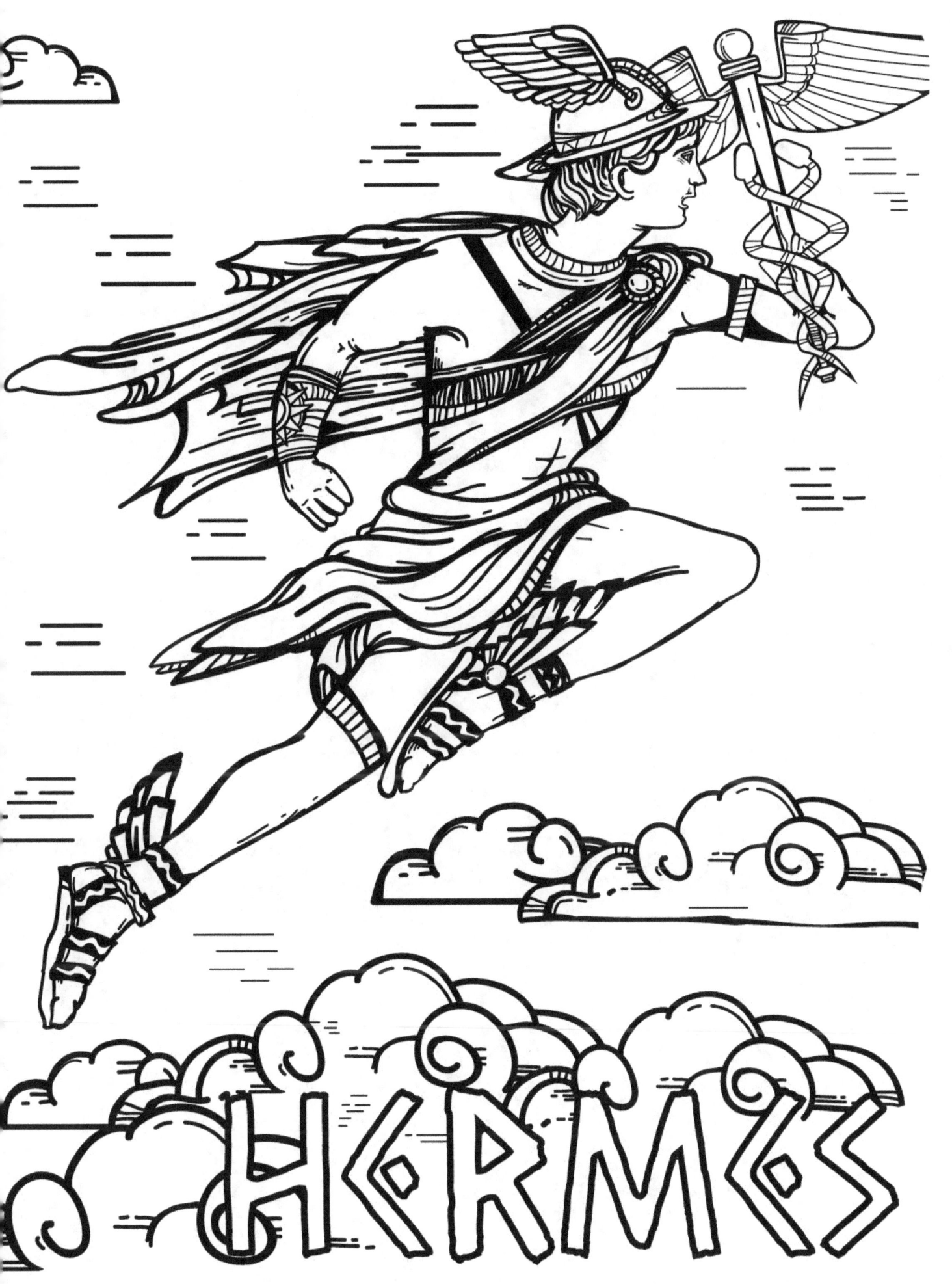

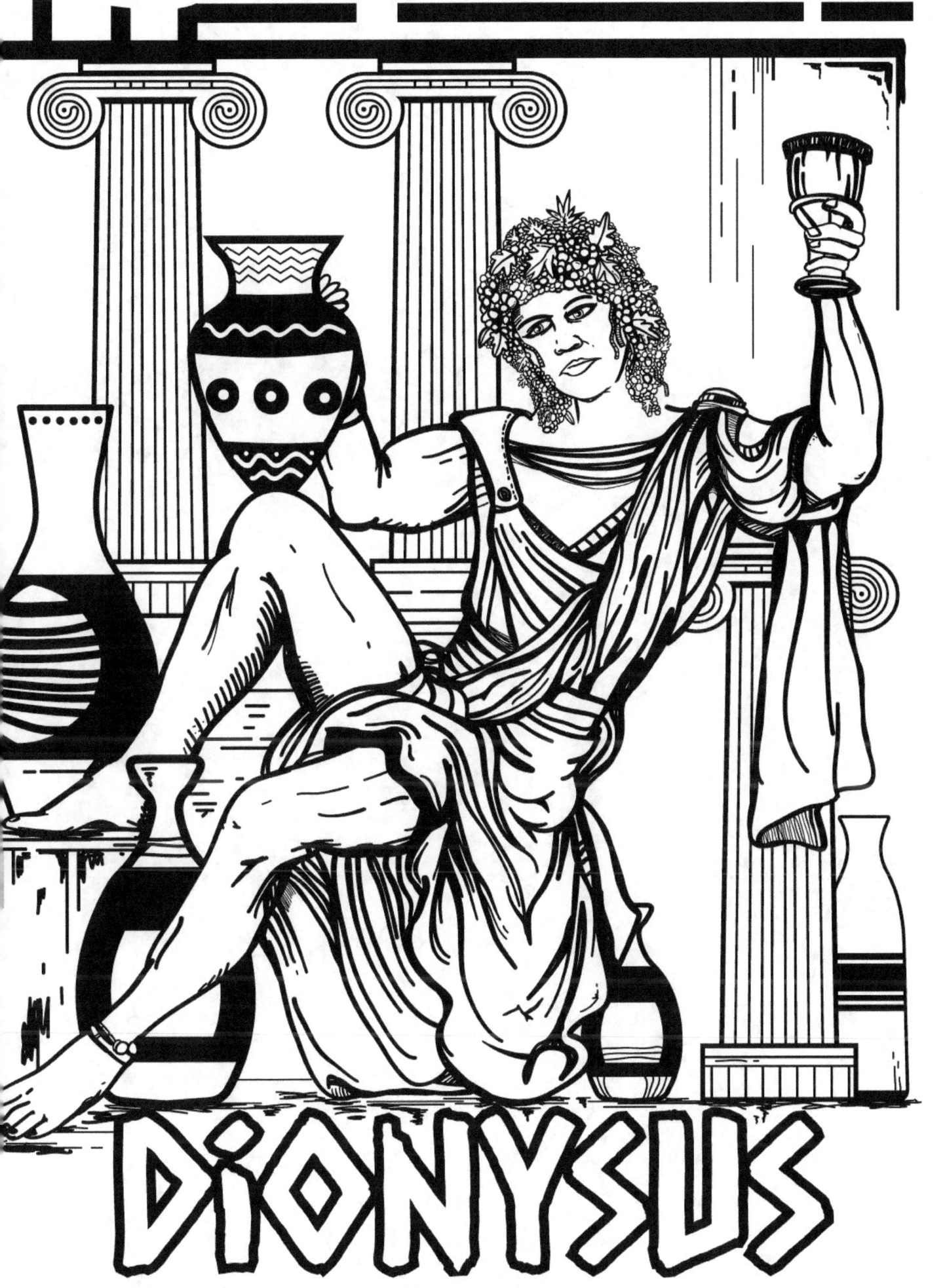

DIONYSUS

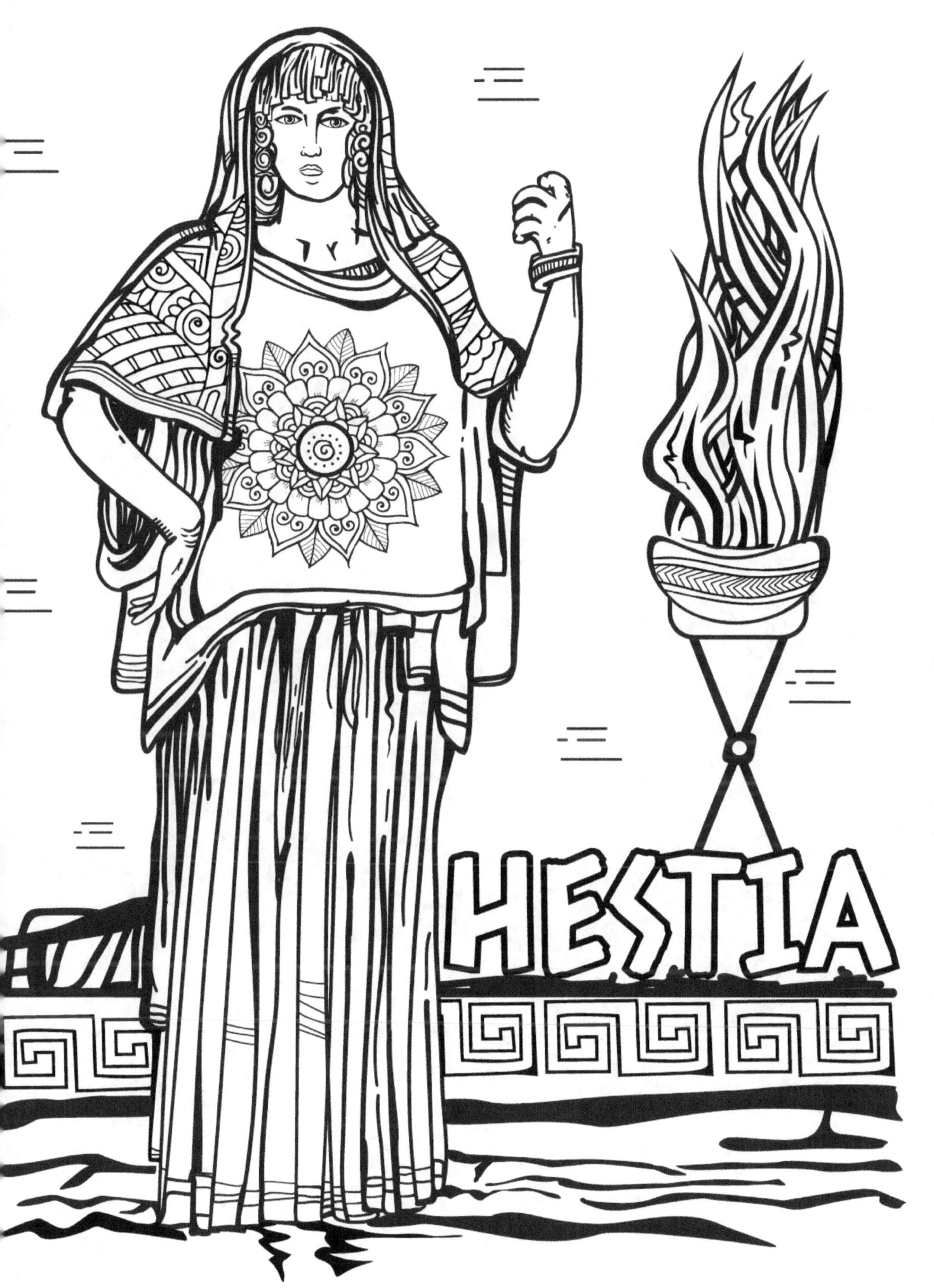

HESTIA

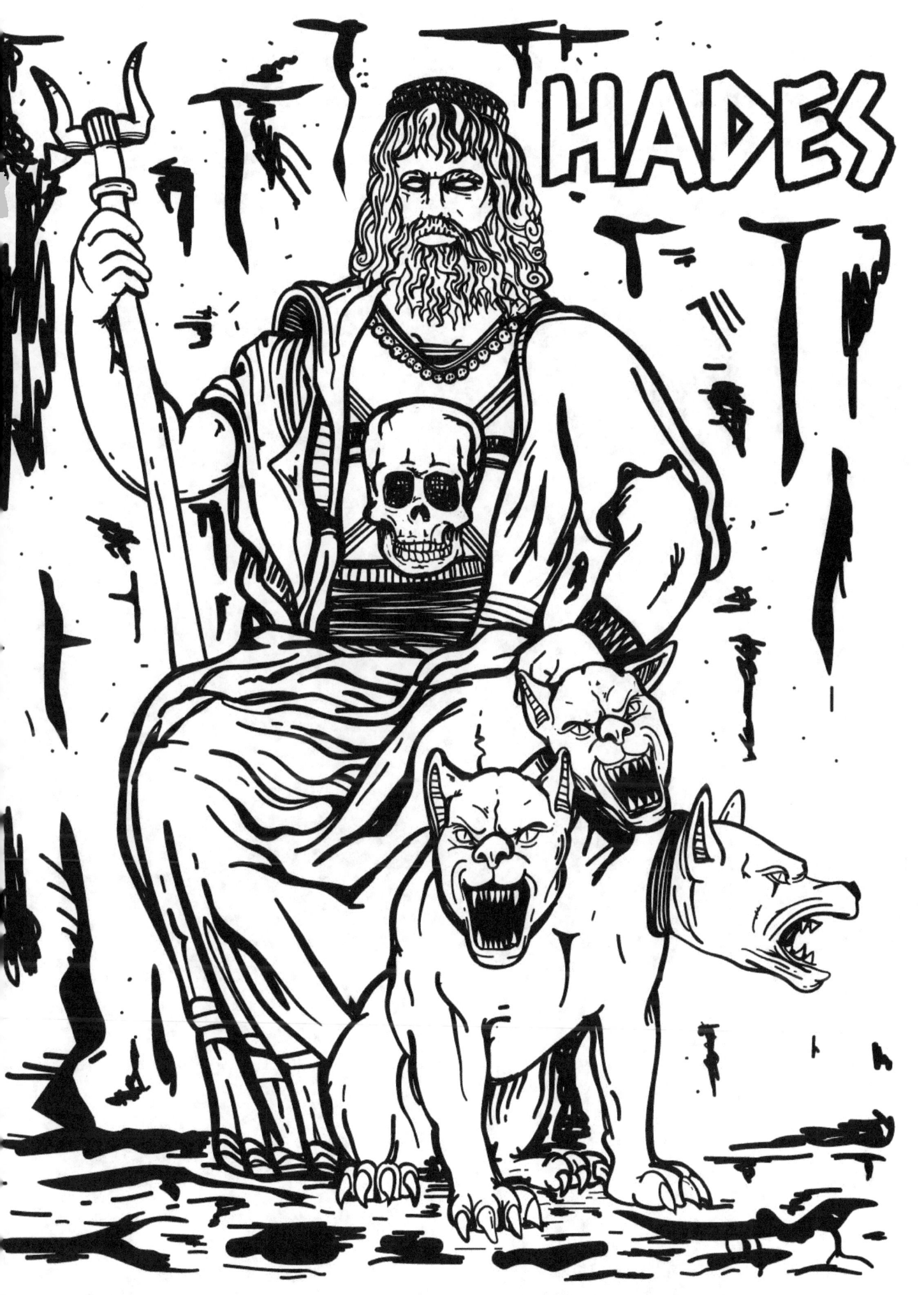

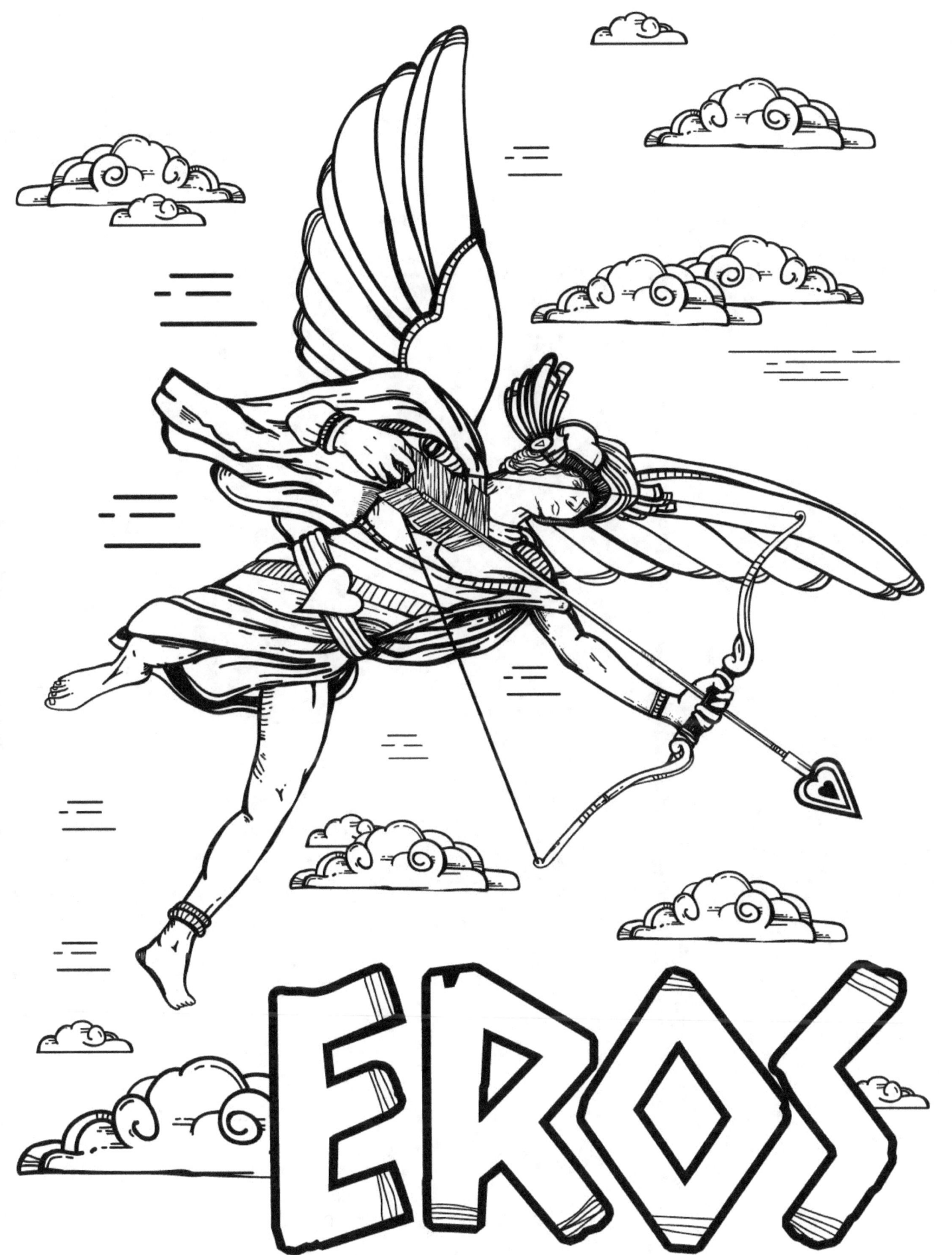

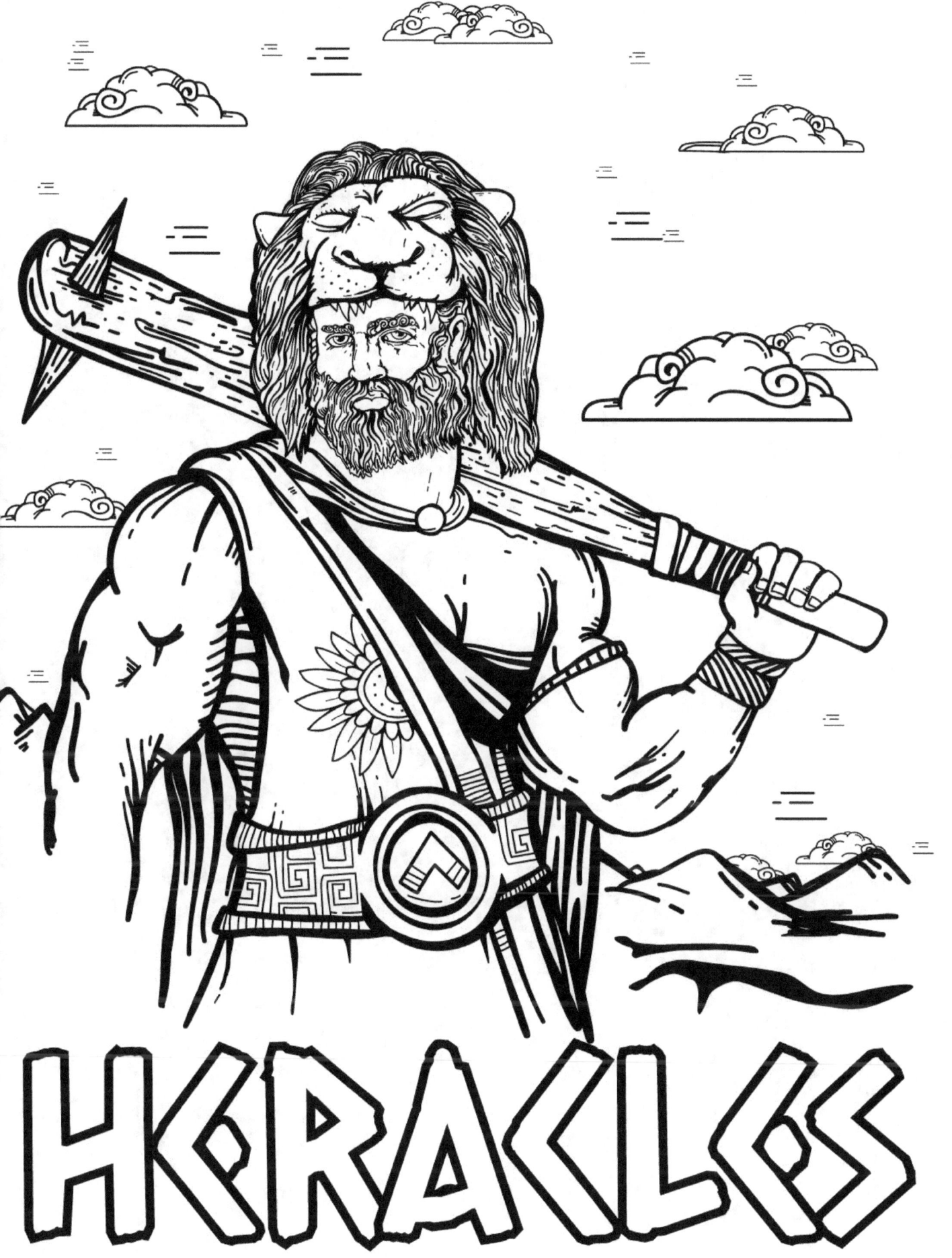

HERACLES

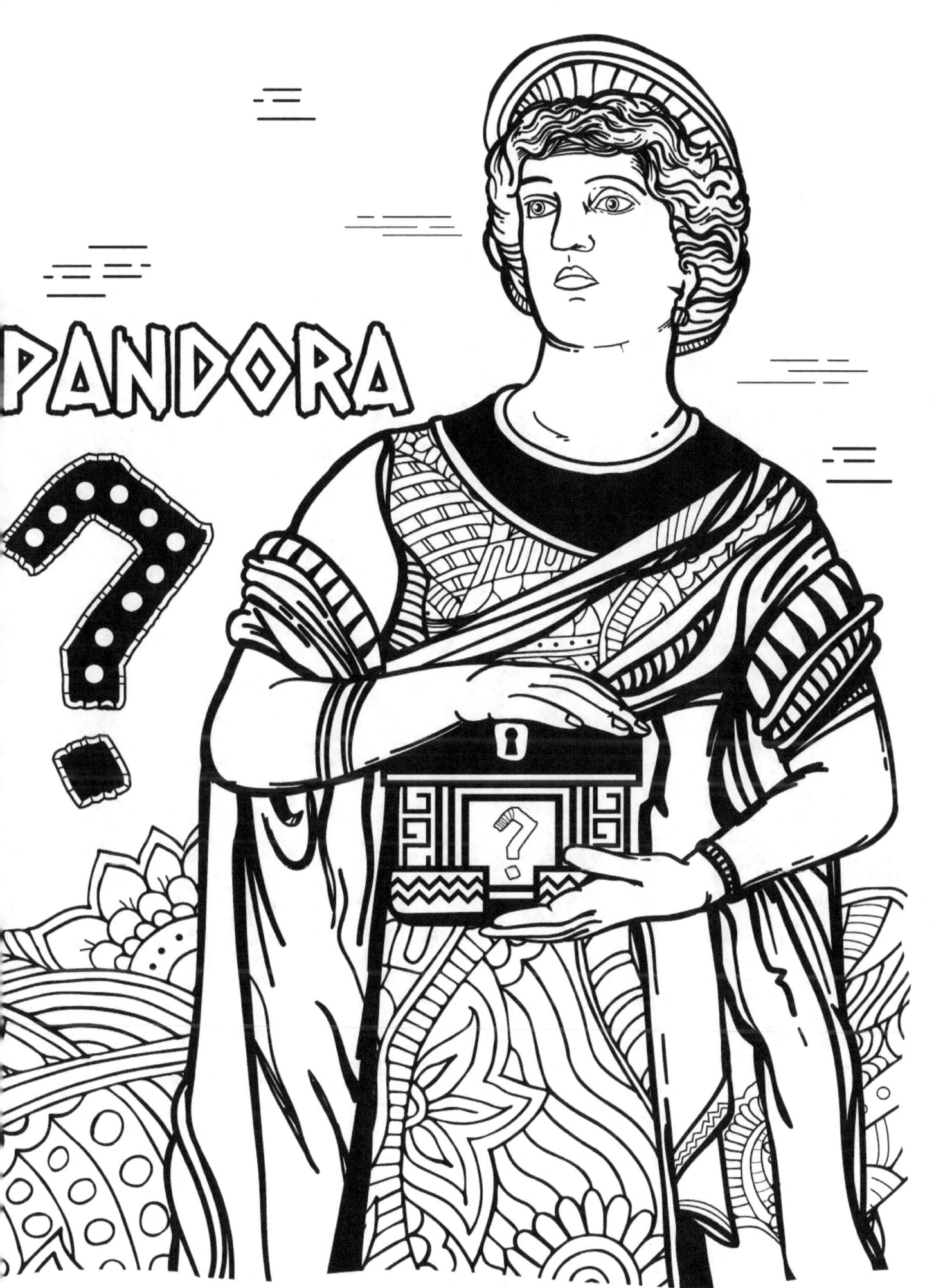

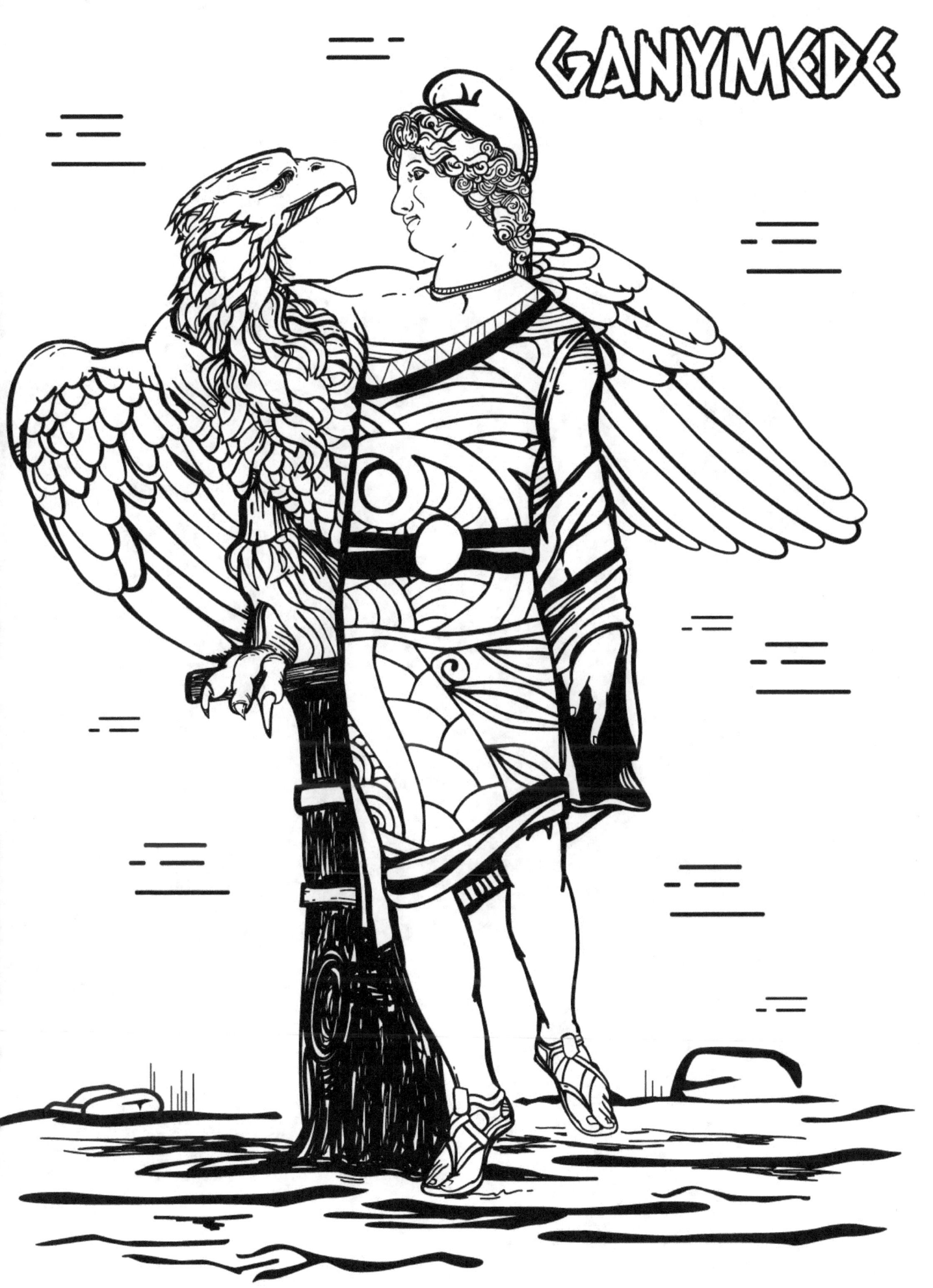

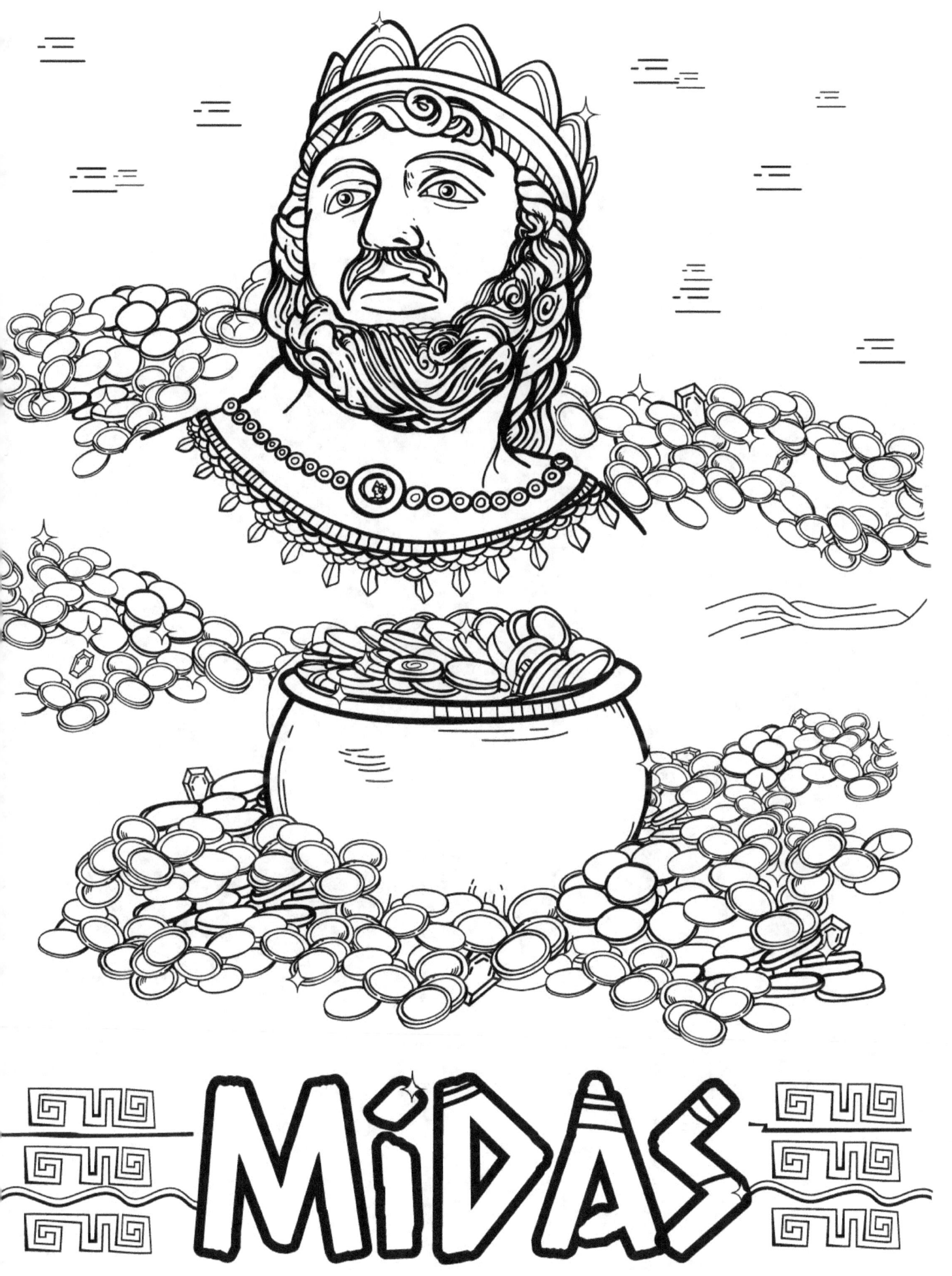

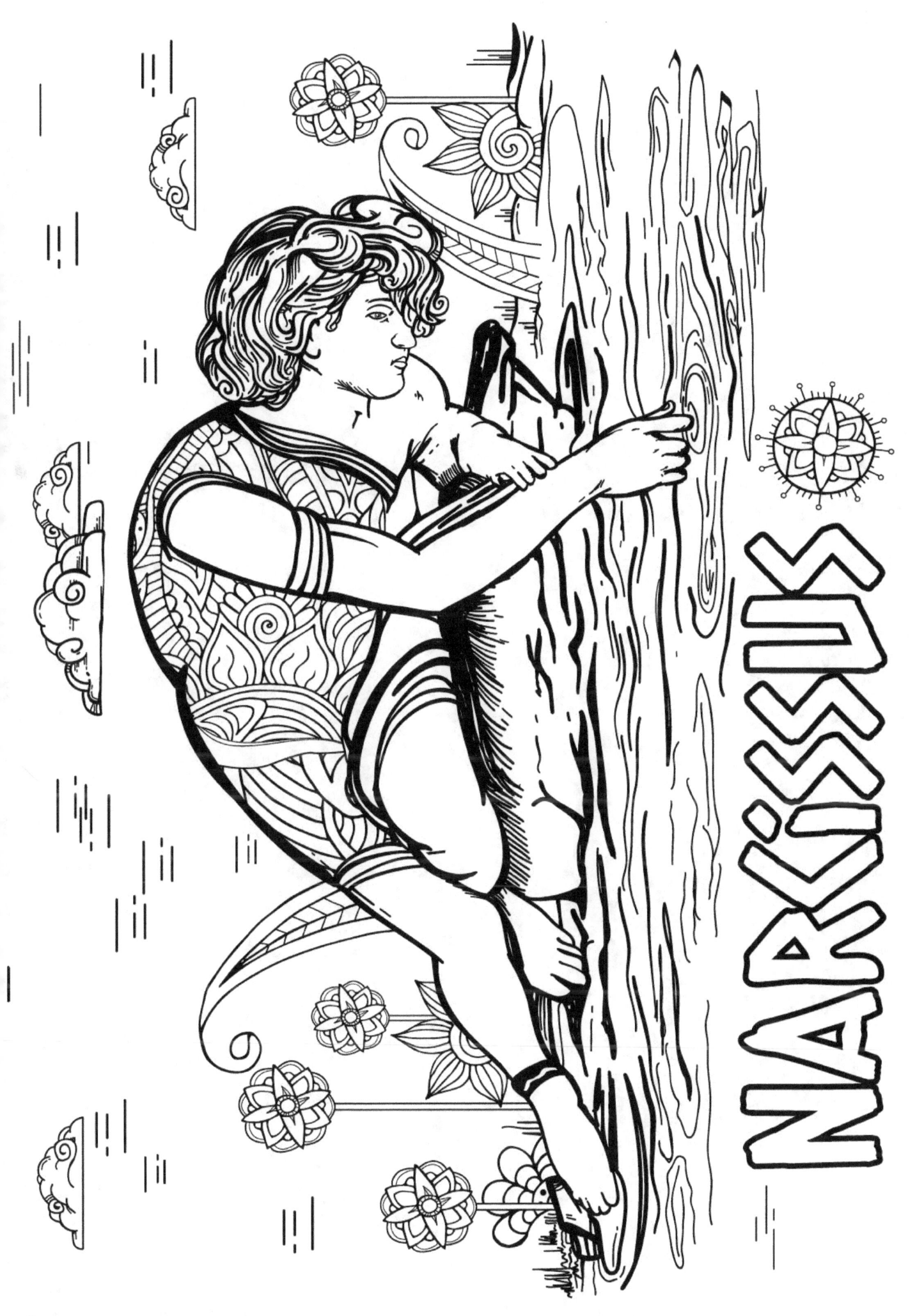

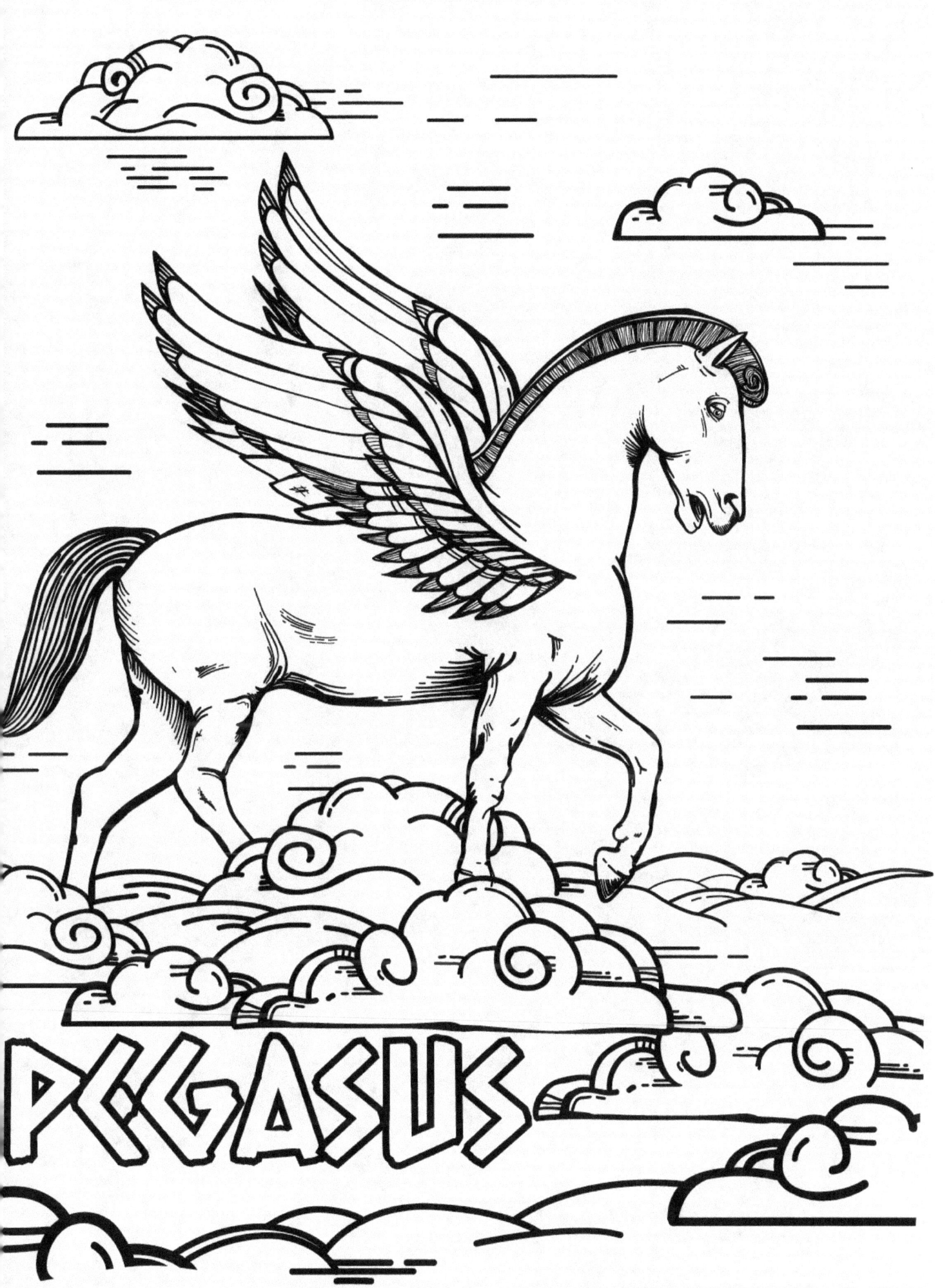

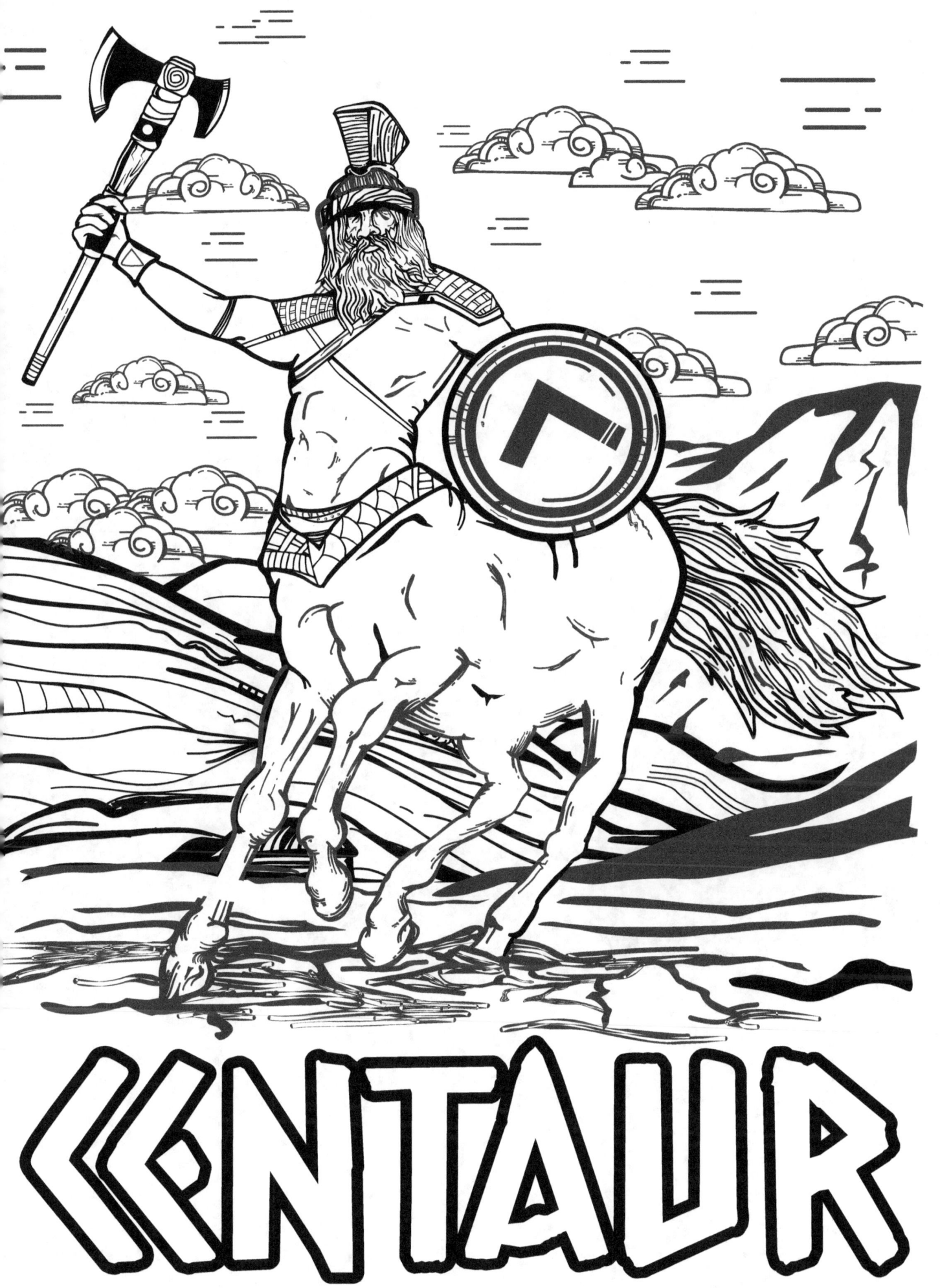

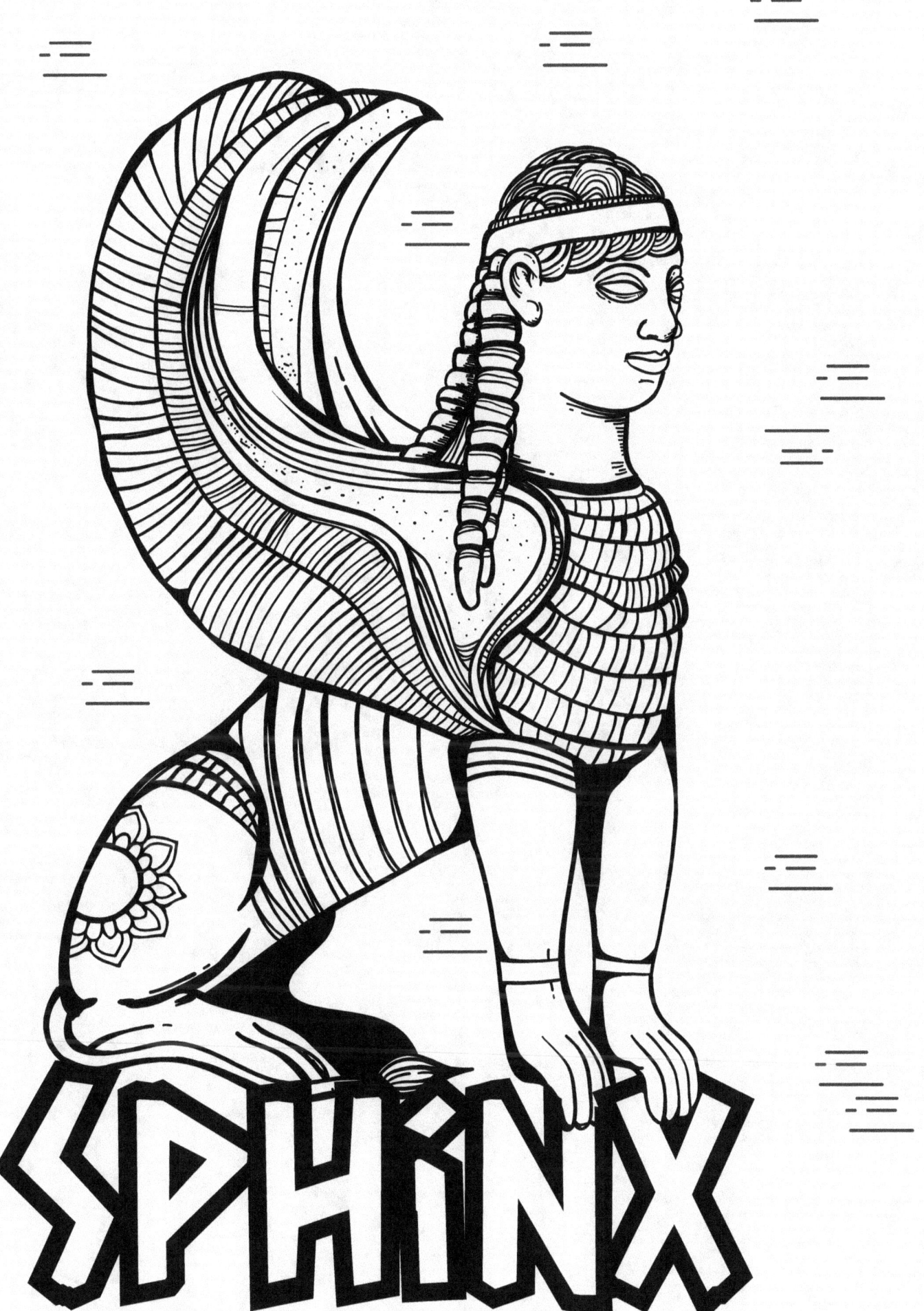

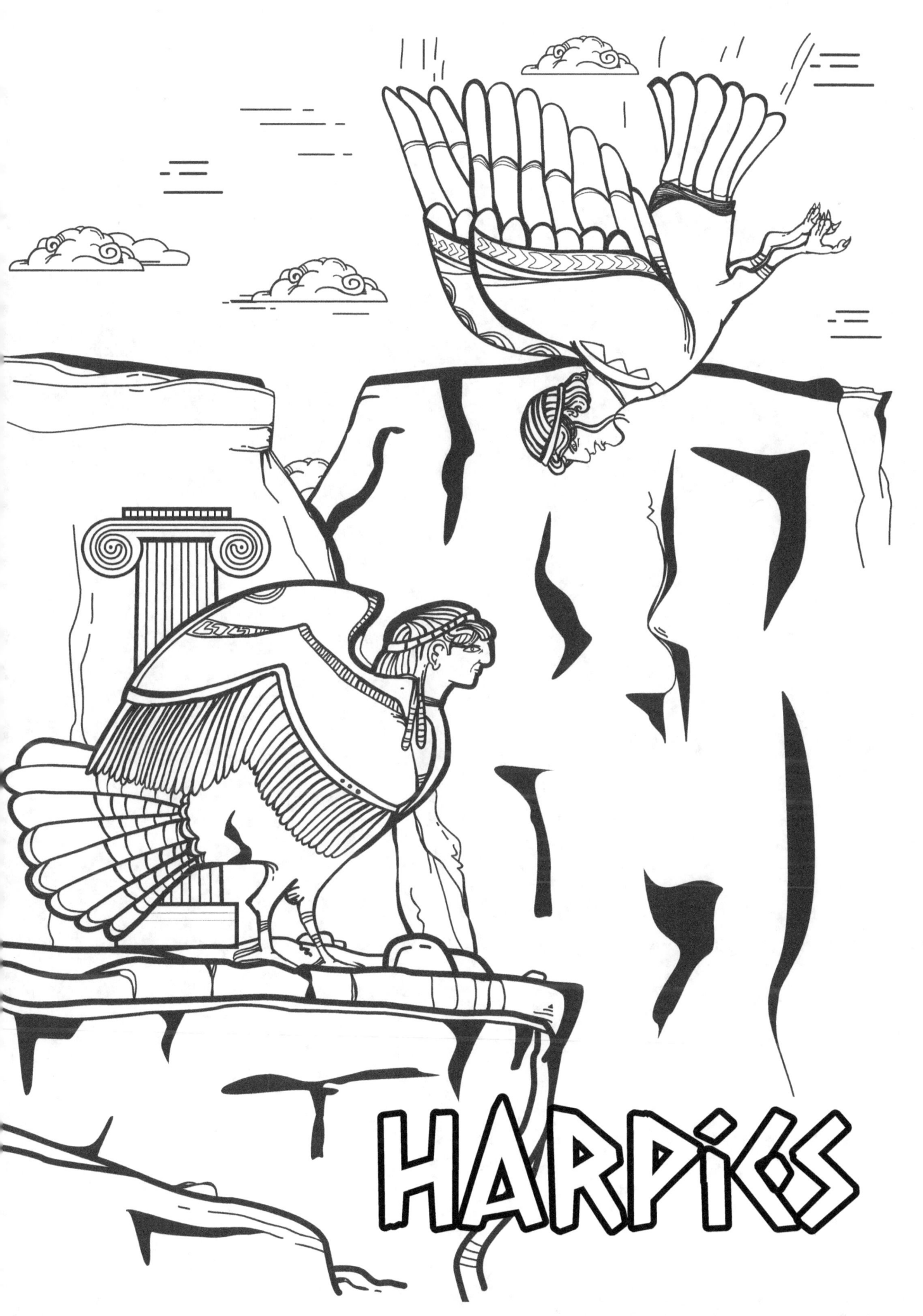

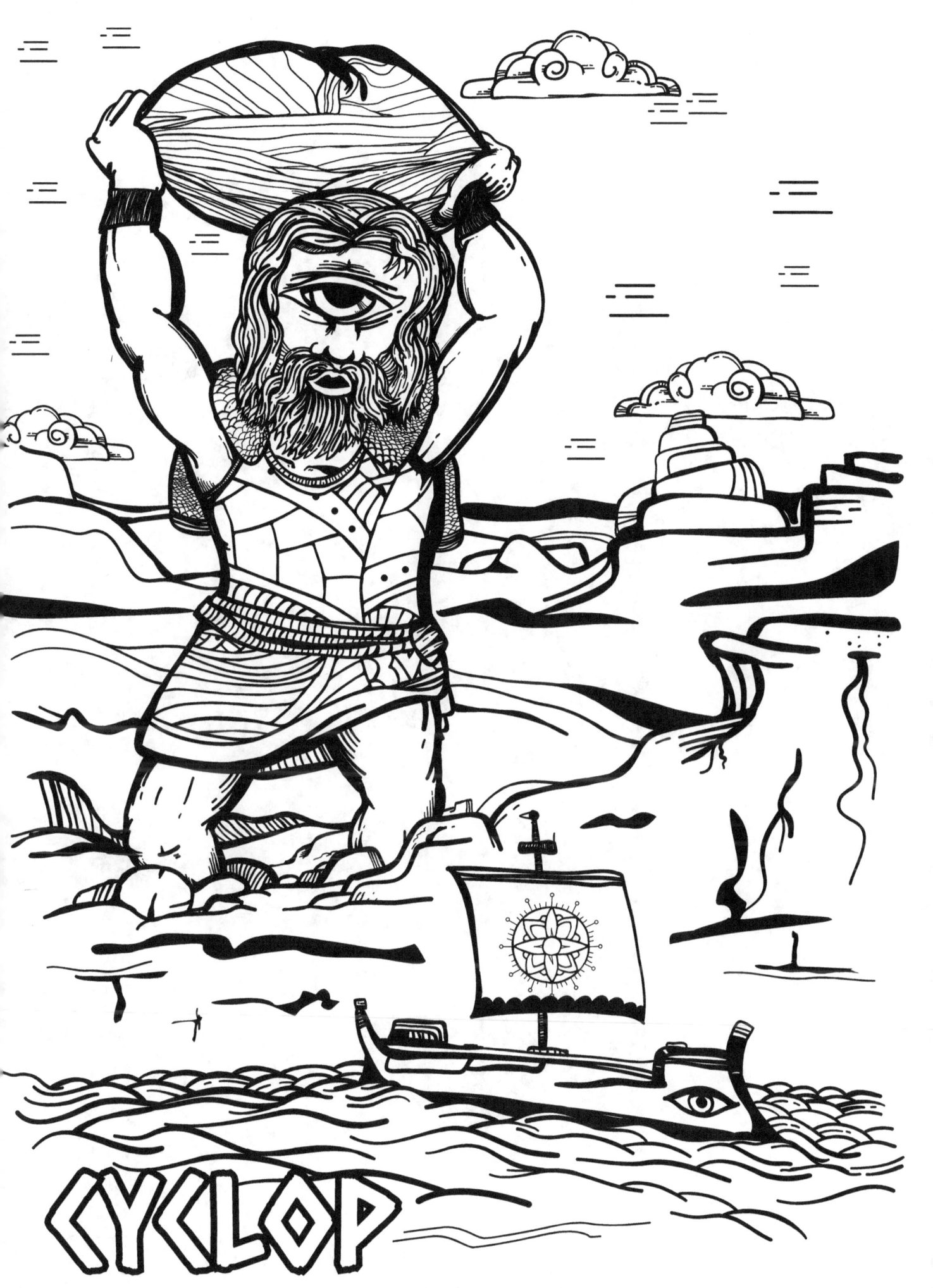

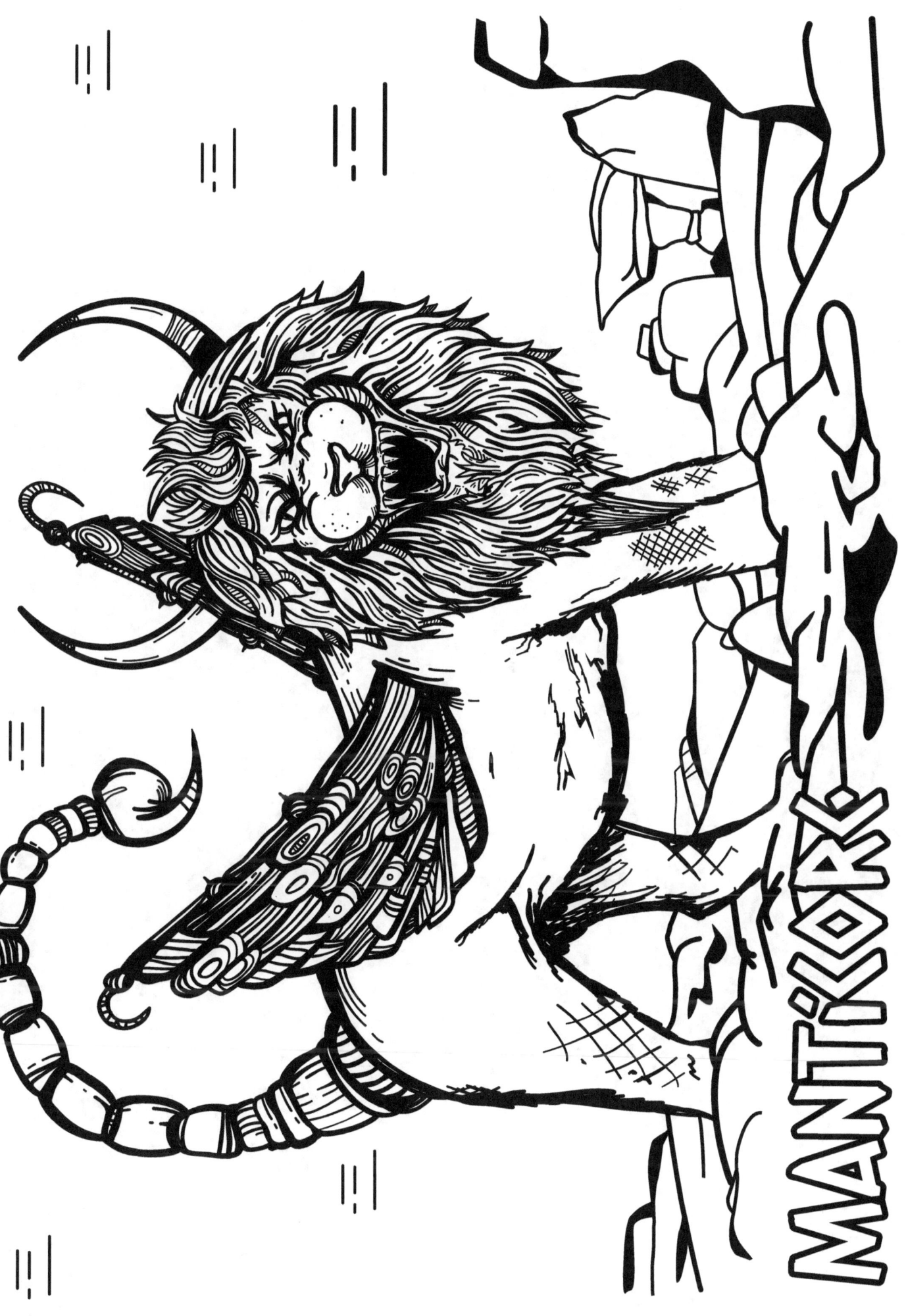

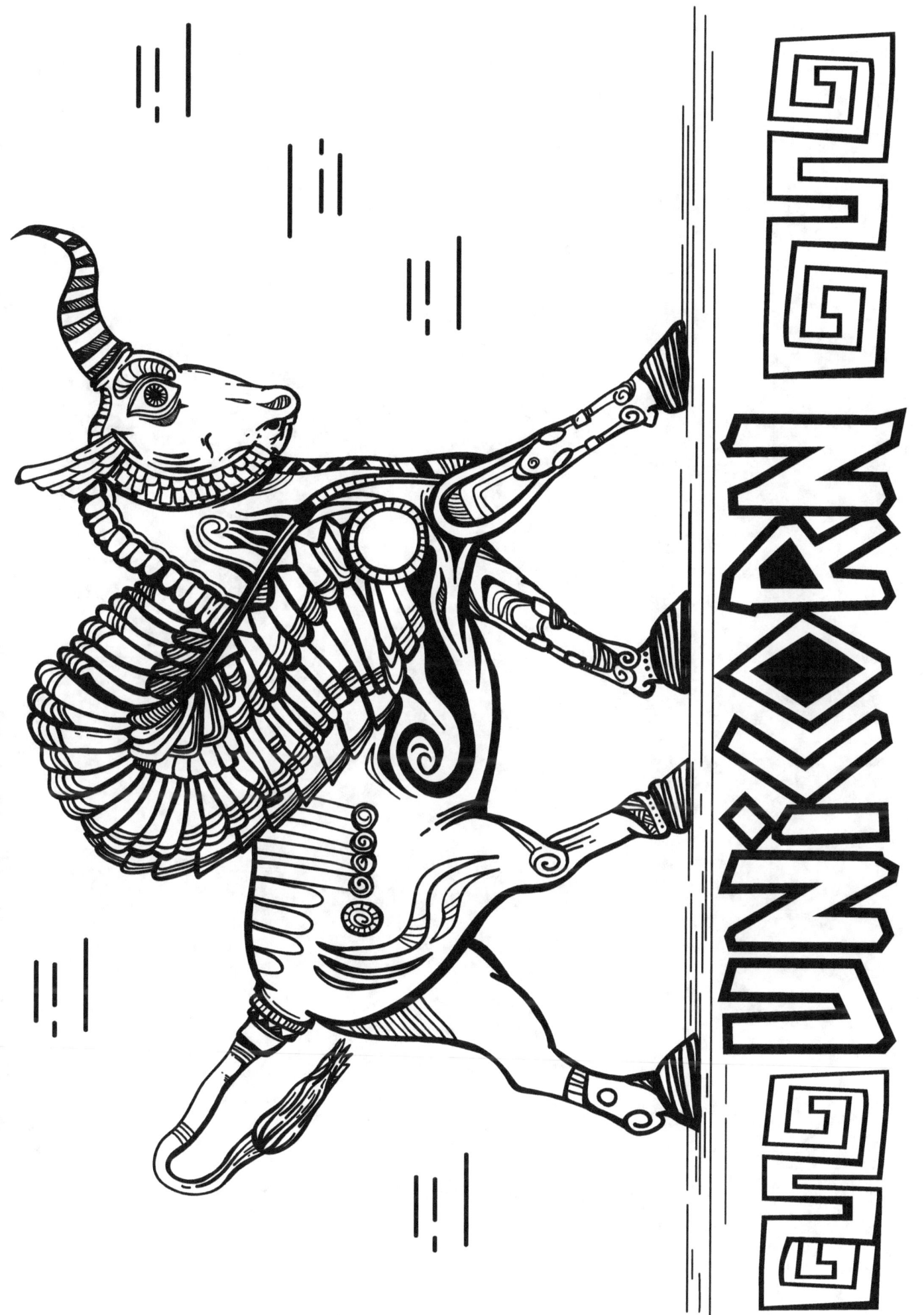

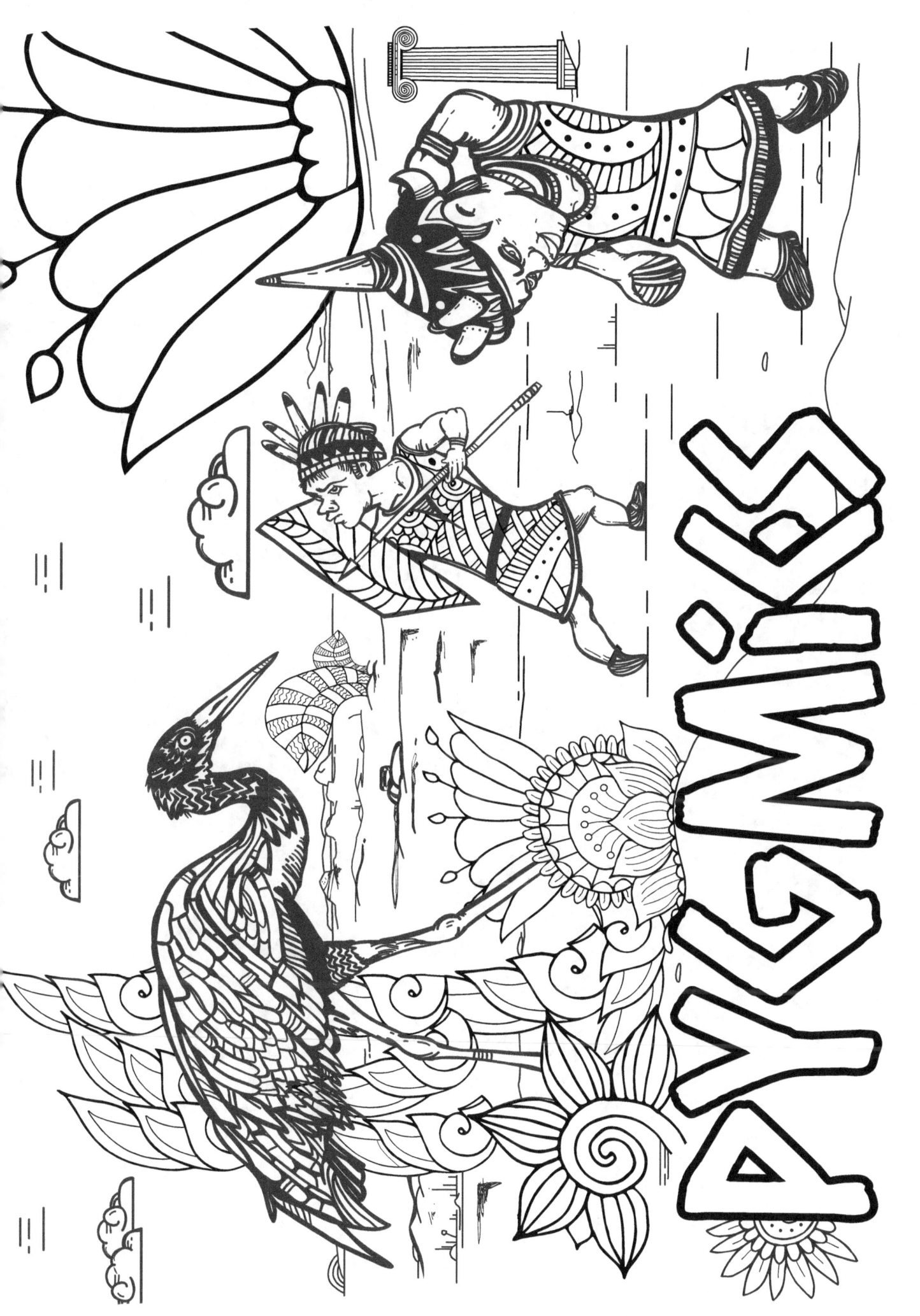

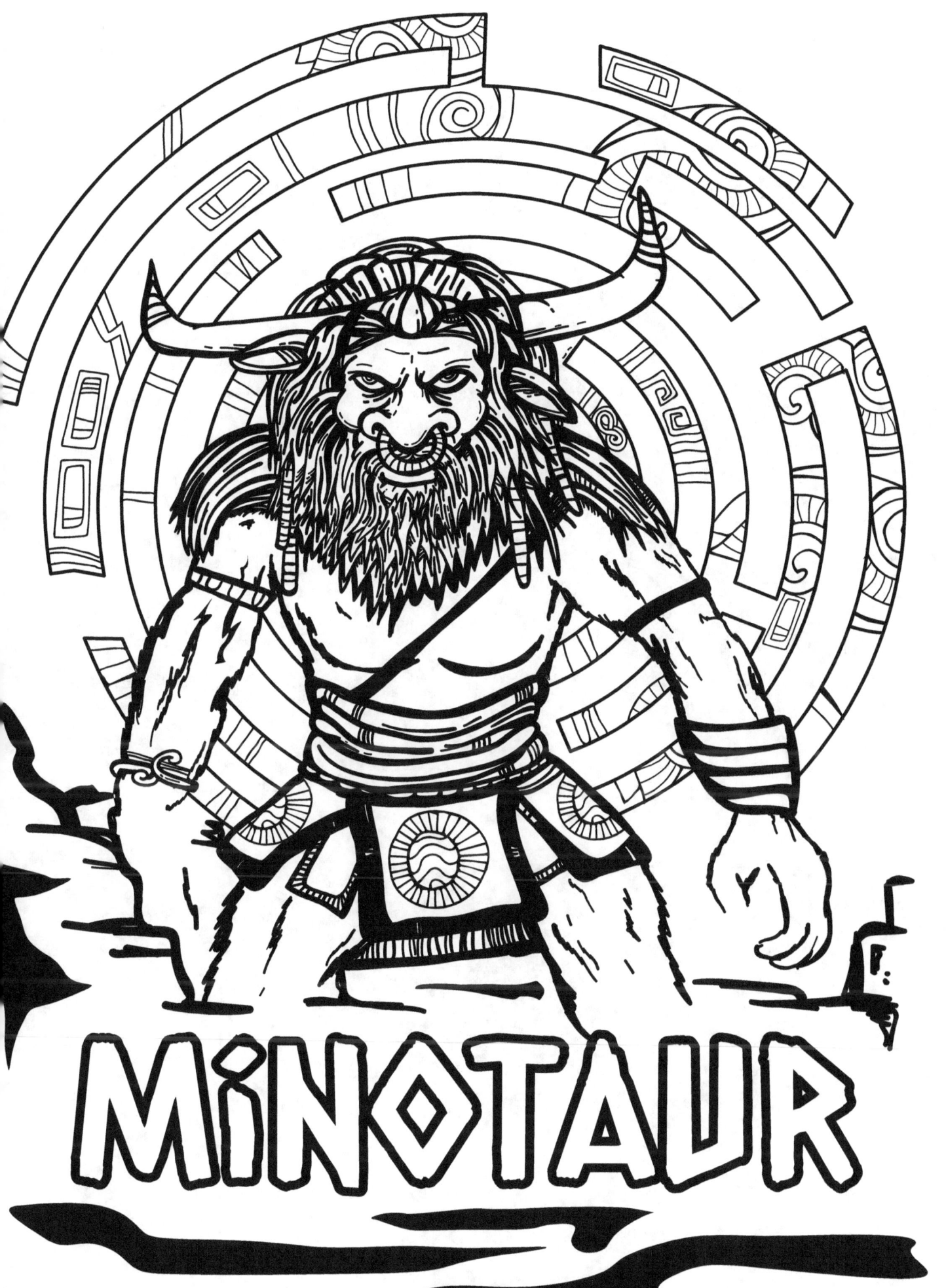

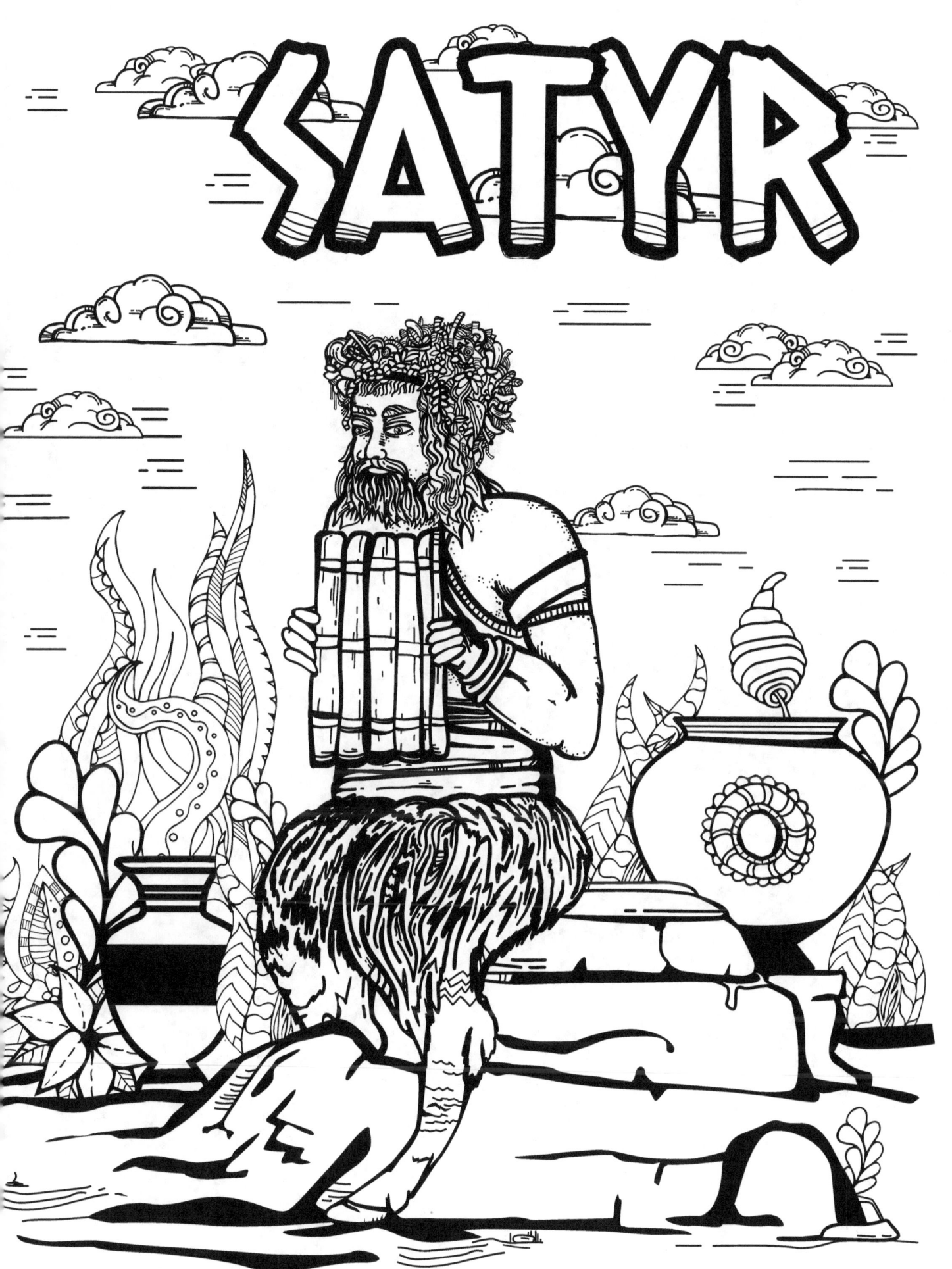

DRAGON

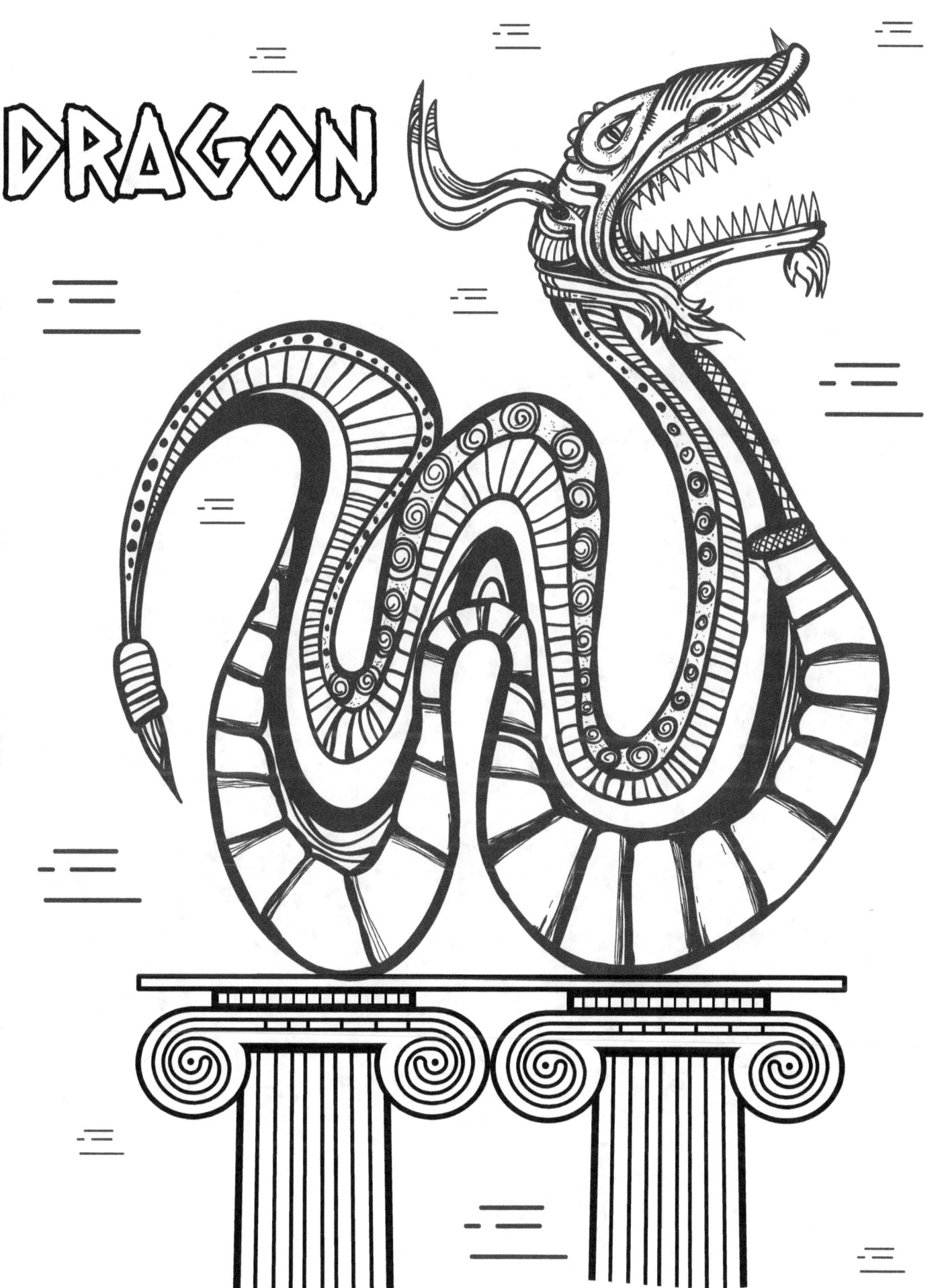

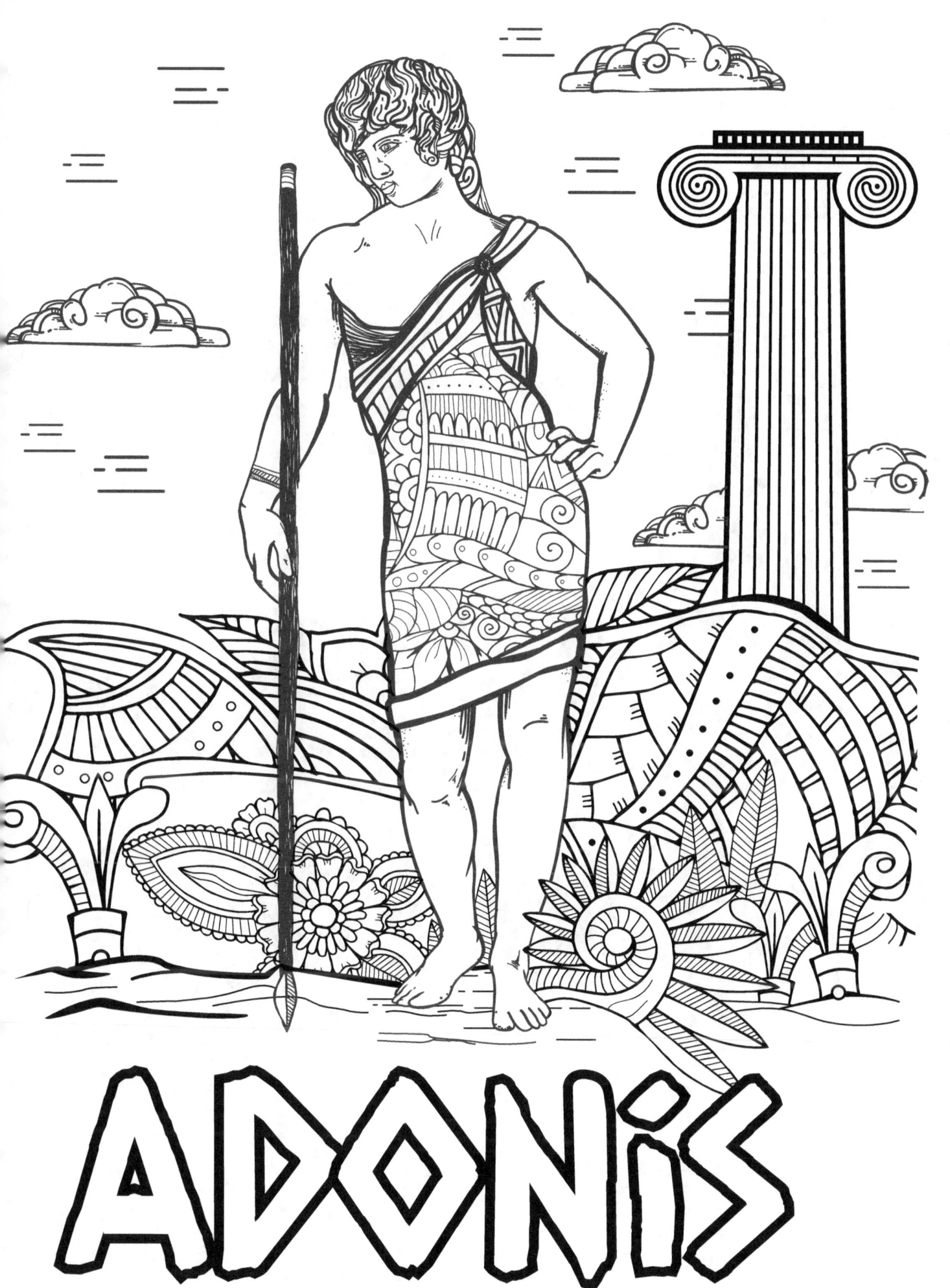

ADONIS

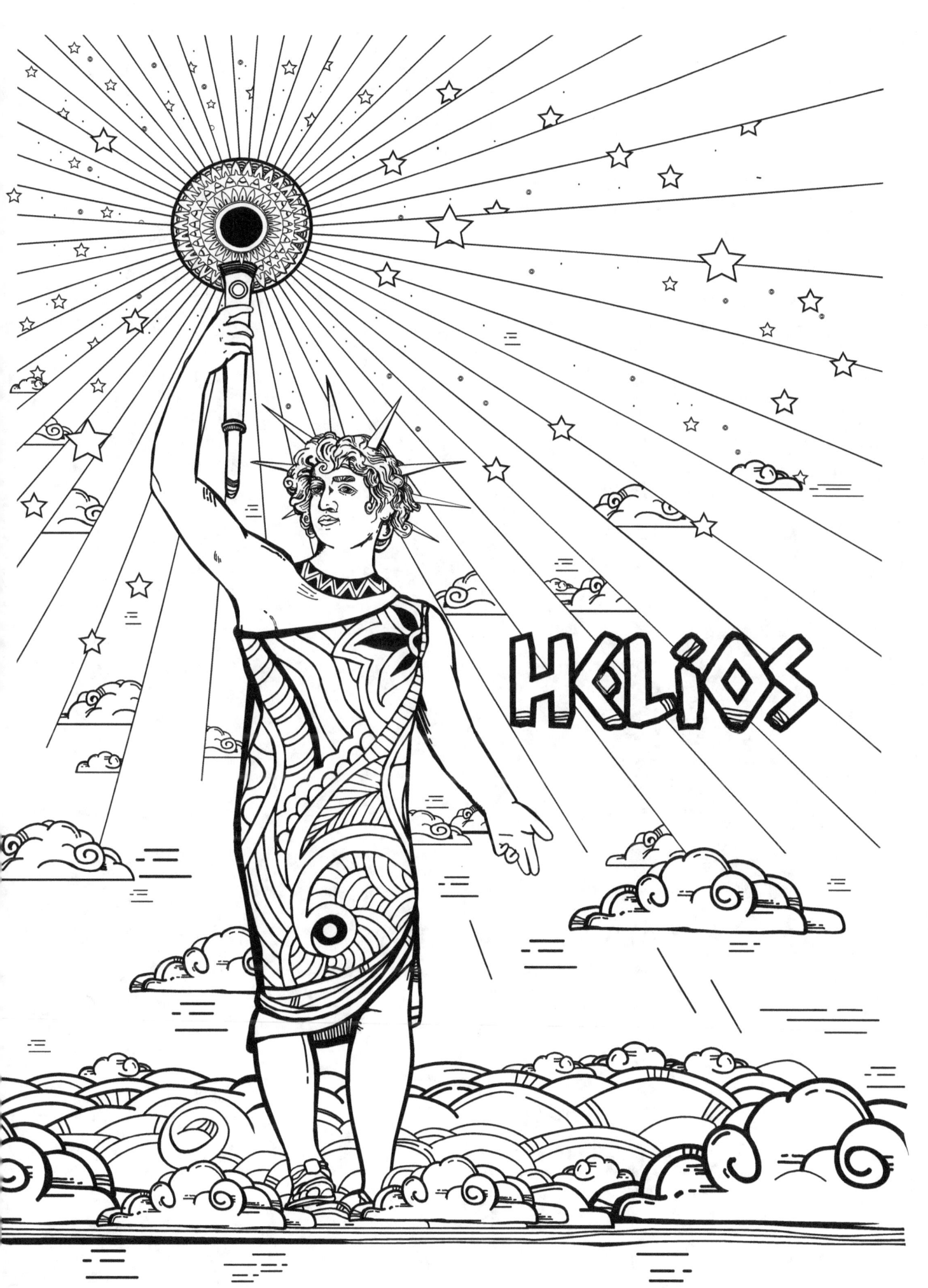

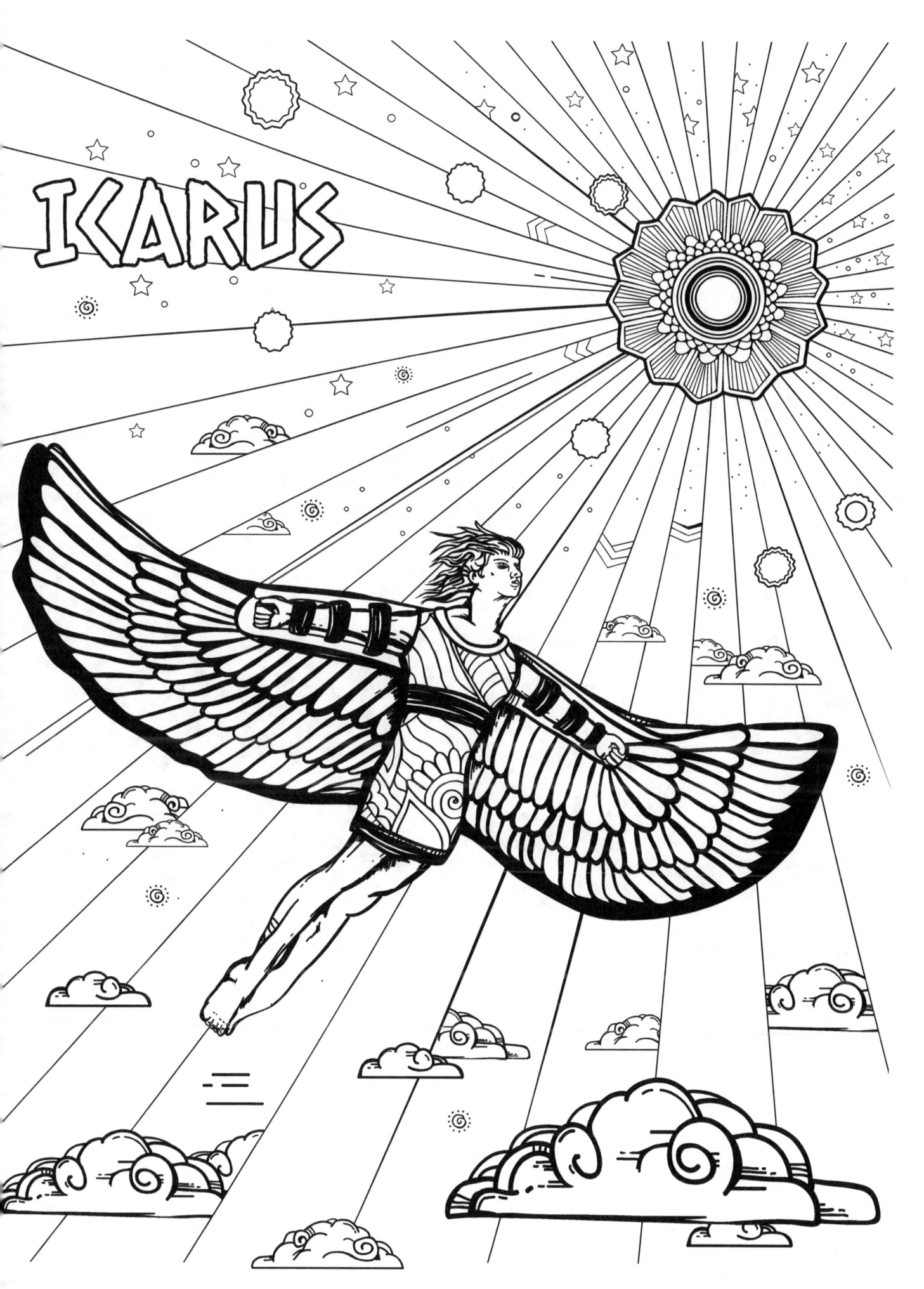

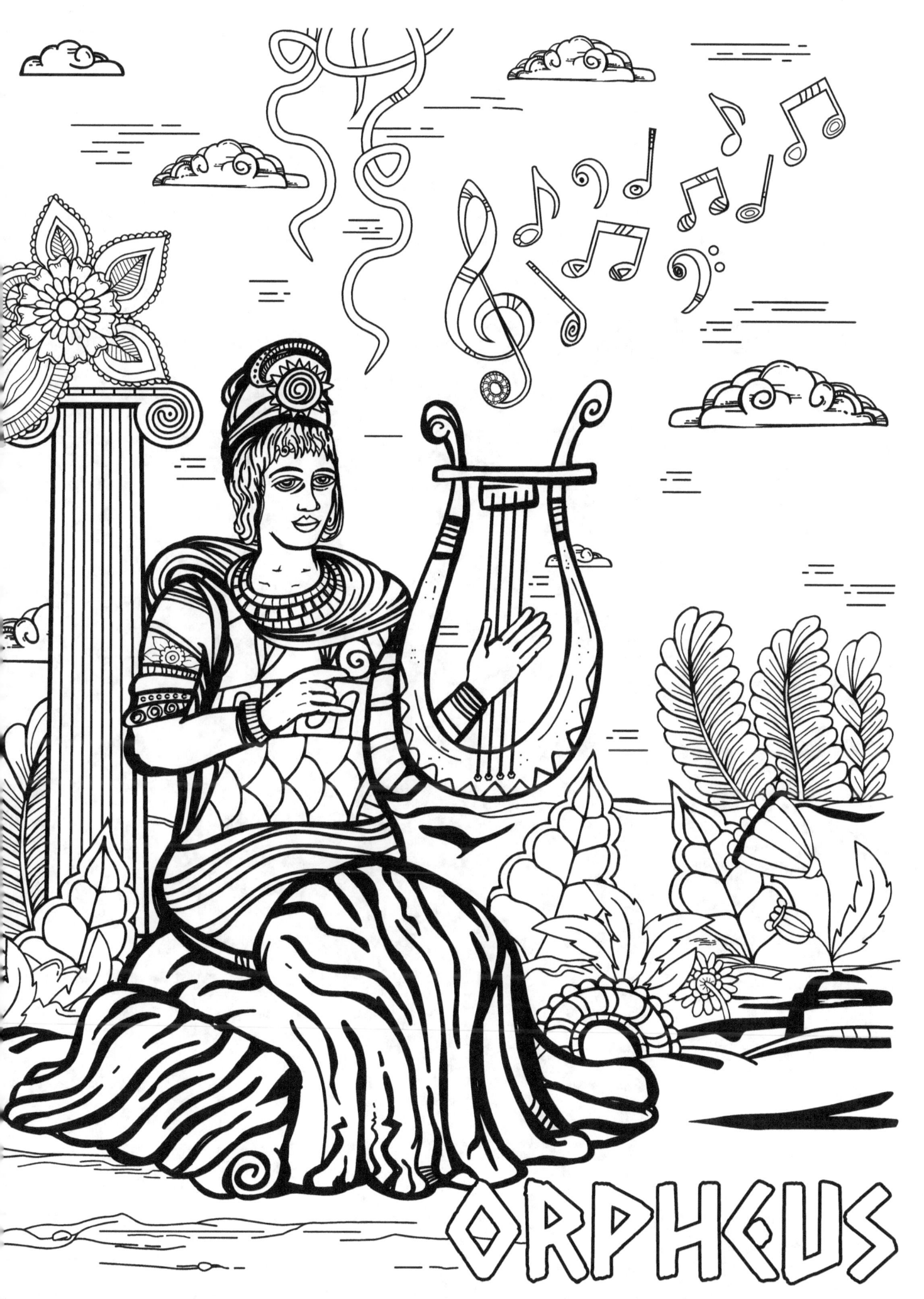

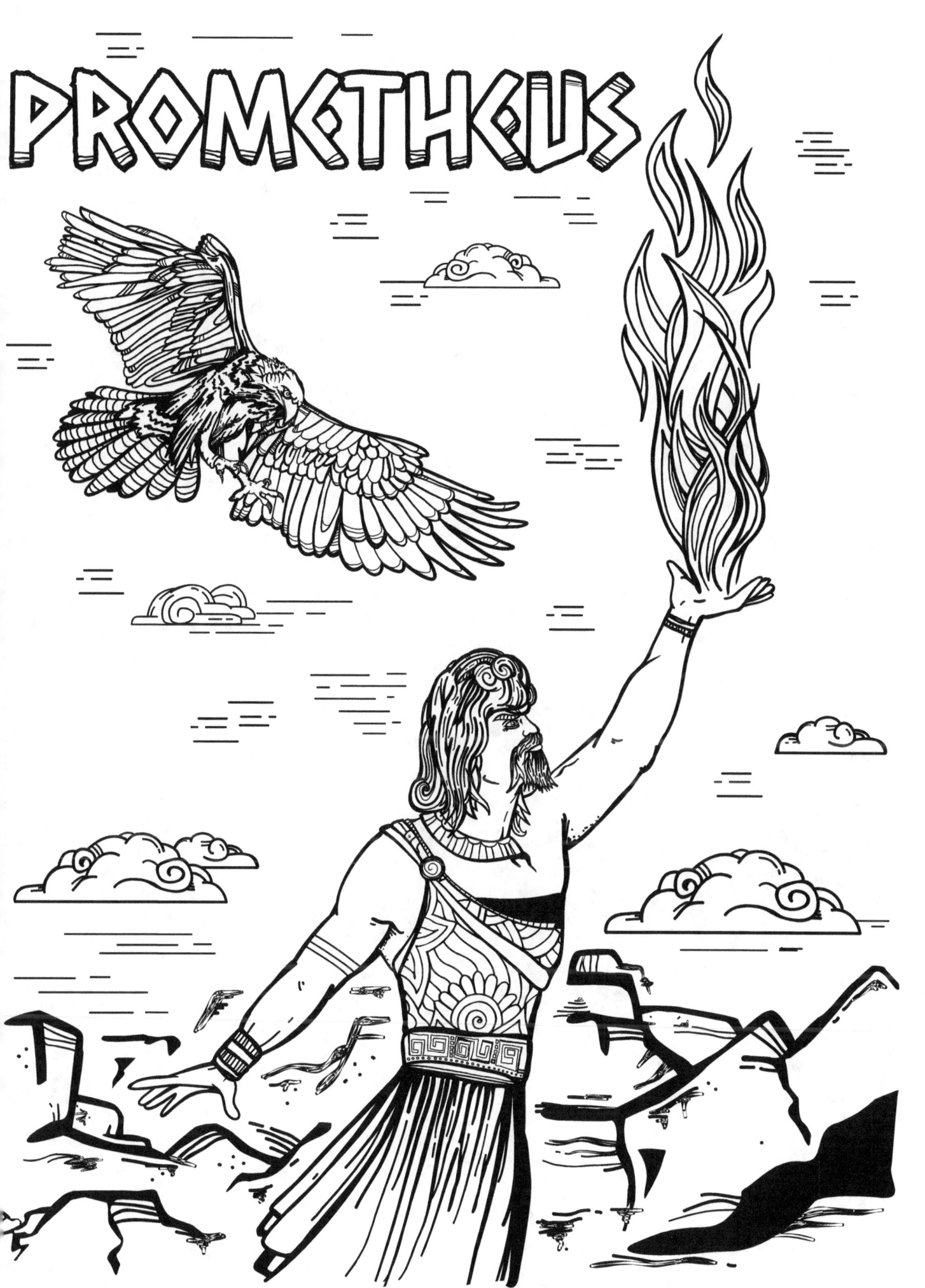

Thank you for purchasing this book.

If you would like to know more about Aryla Publishing Books please visit:-

www.ArylaPublishing.com

Or follow us on
Facebook
Twitter
Instagram
for *free promotions*

@arylapublishing

We would love to know what you think of this book so please leave us a review.

Have a wonderful day

Other Coloring Books from Aryla Publishing

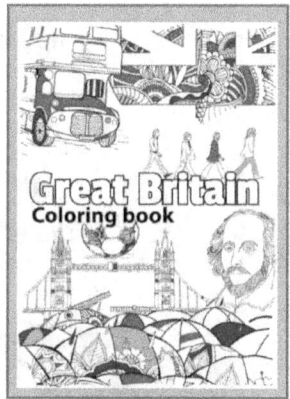
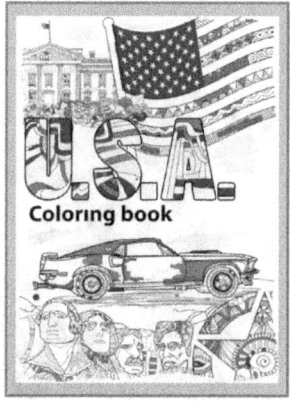
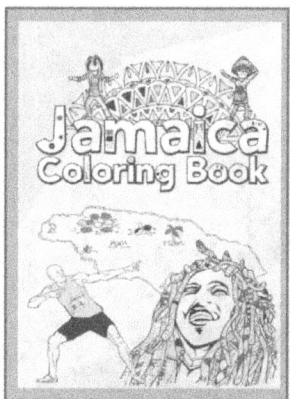
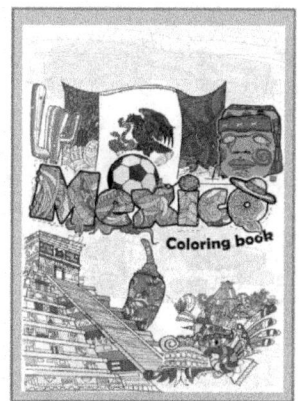

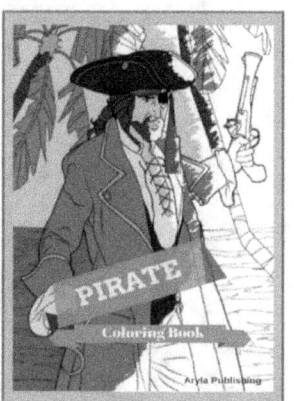
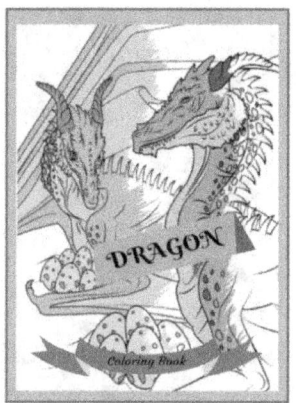
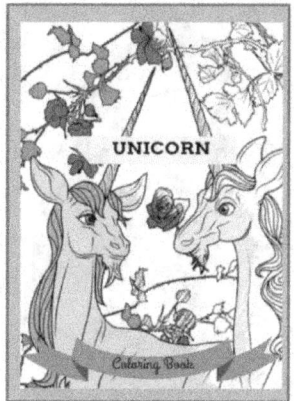
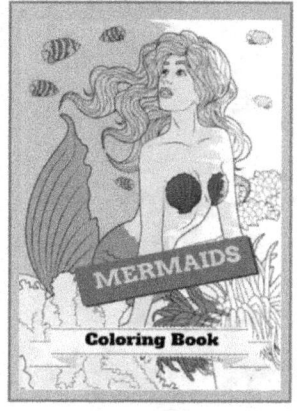

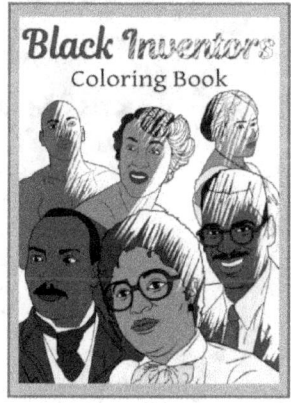
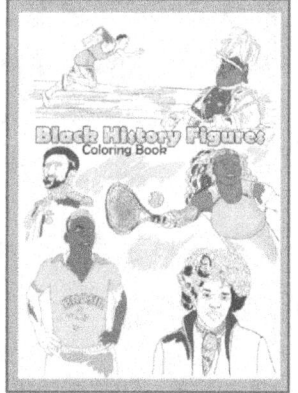
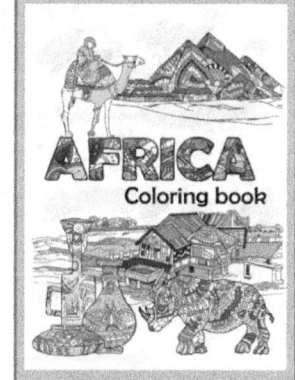
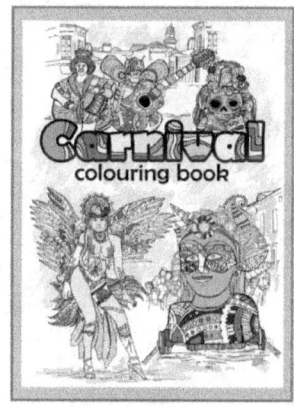

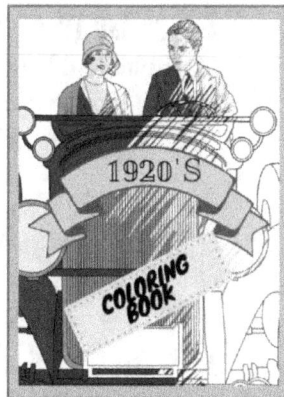
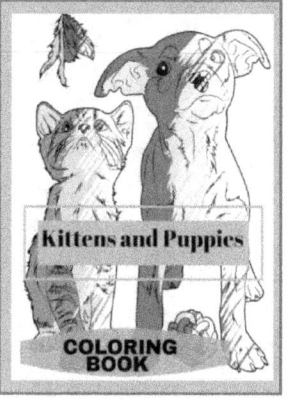
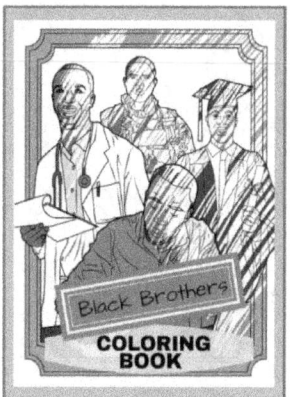
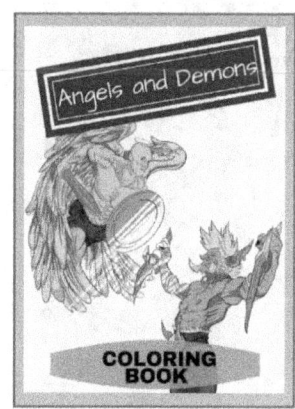

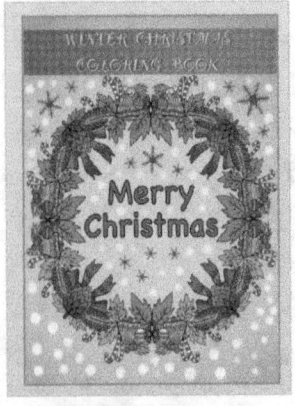

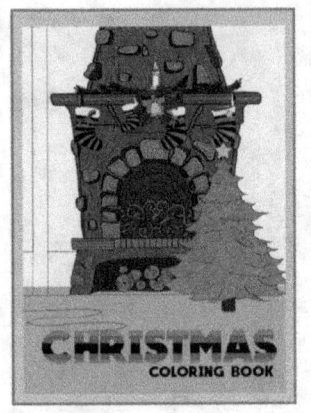
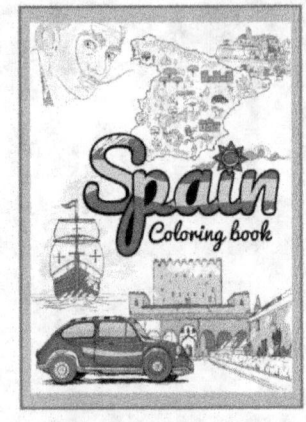
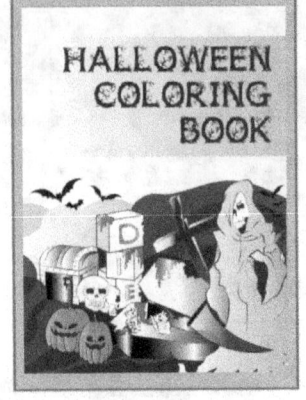
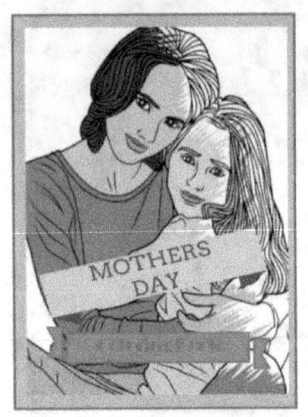
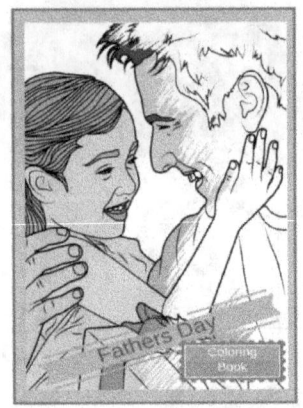
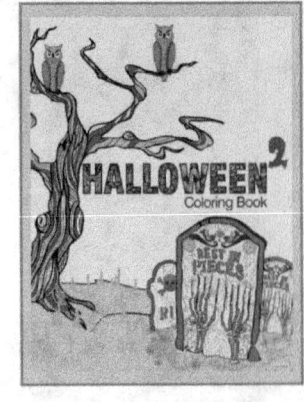
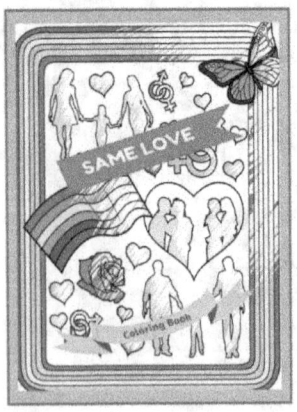
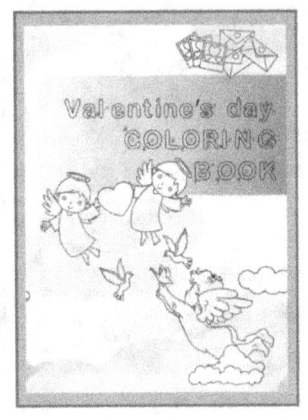
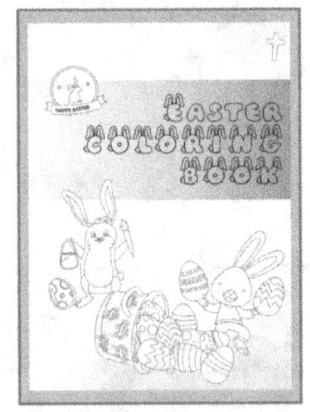
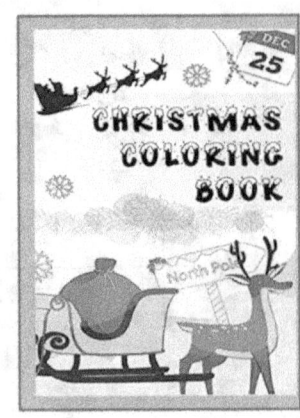
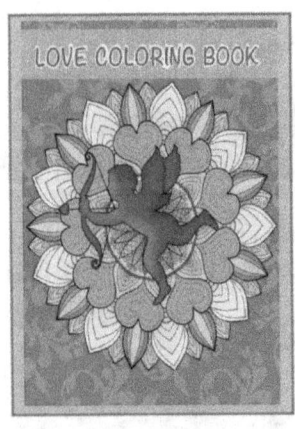
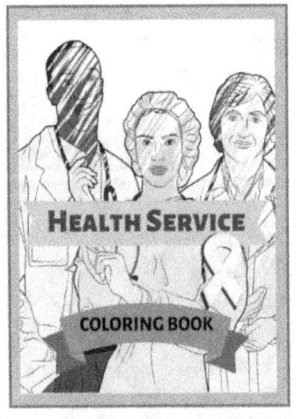
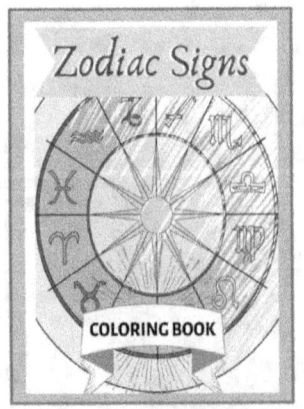
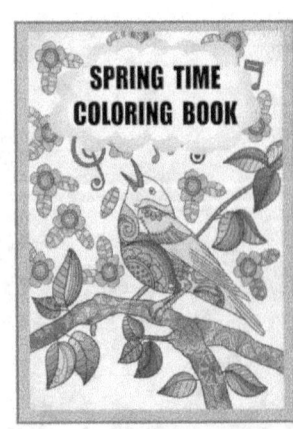

Color In Fun
Kids Books

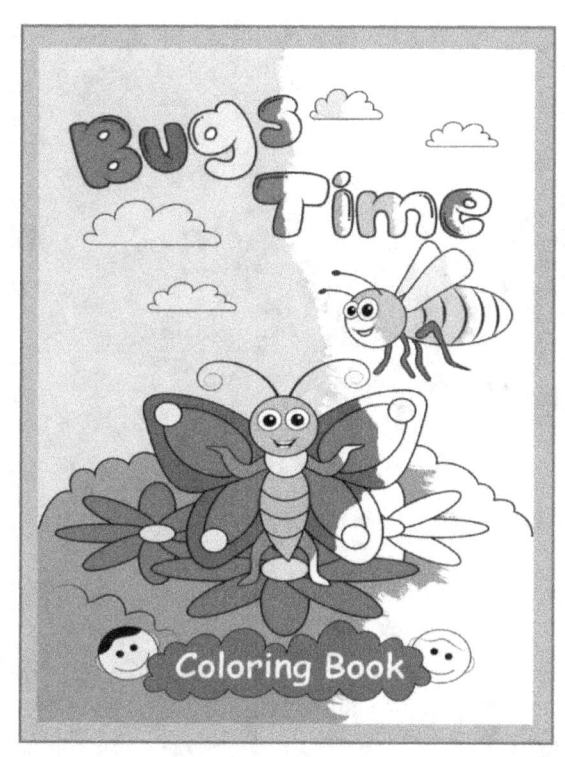

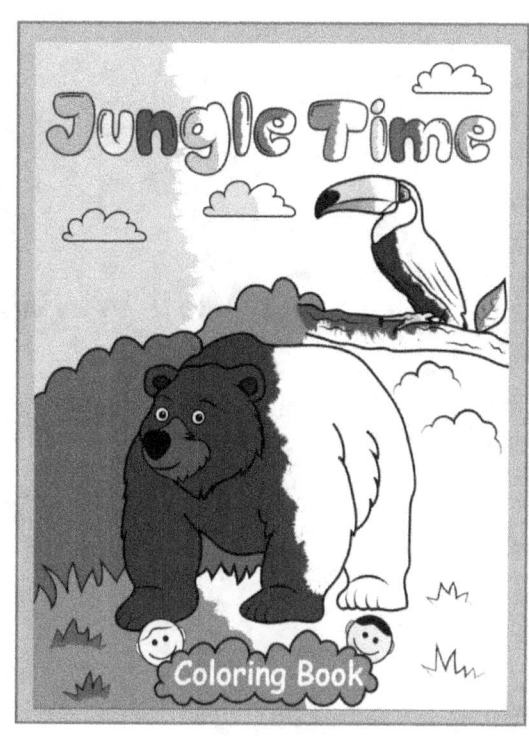

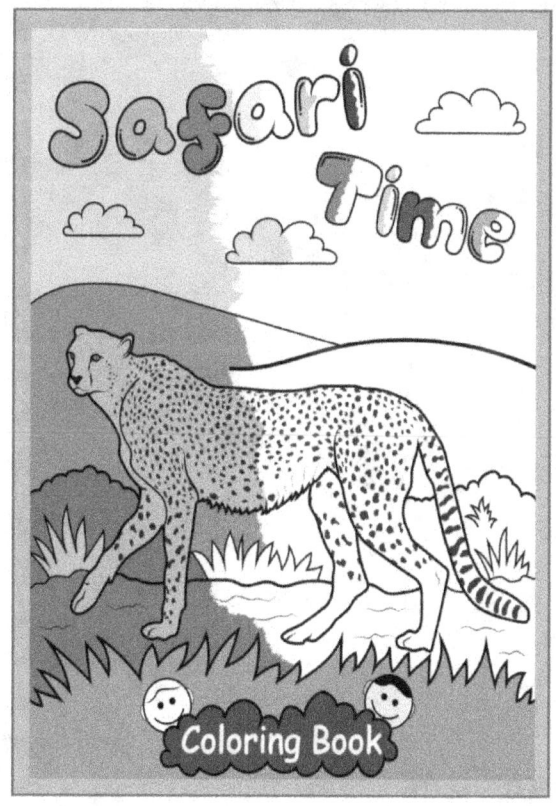

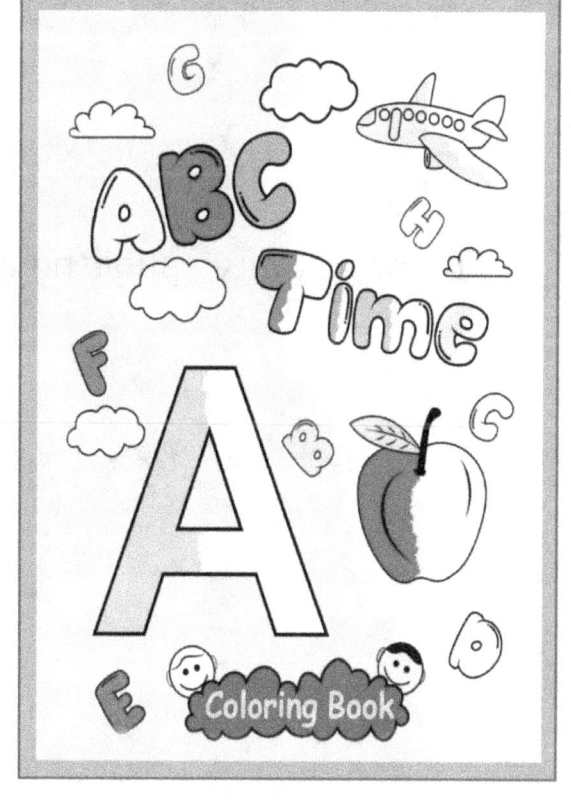

Visit **www.ArylaPublishing.com**
to find out about all new releases.

Follow us @arylapublishing on Twitter Instagram & Facebook

Search for Aryla Publishing on

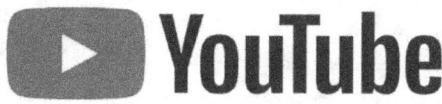 **YouTube**

Check out our <u>Book Trailers</u>

<u>Subscribe</u> to keep up to date with new releases!